The Ruth Kazez Swim Workbook
Practical workouts & technique

Ruth Talman Kazez
edited by Rachel Hannah Kazez

Art by Ruth Talman Kazez

Forward

Four decades ago, at age 50, Ruth Talman Kazez took up swimming again after the kids had moved out of the house. This soon took her to masters-level wins in butterfly, then to Ironmans and triathlon World Championships around the world. Two decades ago (around 2000), she started writing about swimming and posting workouts on her website. The website took off. She'd often see strangers using her workouts in the lane next to her at the pool, and I've had friends ask if I know someone with my last name, named Ruth, who writes such great—and still ubiquitous—swim workouts for people at all levels, beginner to professional.

Now, Ruth wants her workouts and guidance to be consolidated into a book, with help from her granddaughters and daughter. Thanks to Becky Groves (granddaughter) for curating the images in the text, and thanks to Jean Kazez (daughter) for her coordination and typing the appendix.

"I want it to be useful," Ruth says. "Something totally practical. This isn't about me, it's about the reader. They didn't come to read about me."

Hello, reader! This is about you. We could talk about my grandma all day, but you have some swimming to do.

- Rachel Hannah Kazez (granddaughter)

Contents

Section 1: Getting Started

This book's main objective is to give you easy-to-read workouts and help you understand some of the physical reasons for the way you are swimming and building fitness. Everyone has to start somewhere. This first section will introduce some thoughts about why we swim, starting swimming as an adult, and getting over fears about swimming, before the subsequent sections provide technique tips, drills, and workouts.

Why do we swim?

Maybe you swim to beat the competition, to be impressive, to stay trim, or to have fun with a group. Whatever brings you to the water, there's something in this book for you.

Why do I swim?

I was in Lake Michigan before I could walk. I remember crawling along the edge of the water and letting my feet go up so that I began crawling on only my hands. Later, when I was older, I watched the lifeguards and copied them. That was a way to learn to swim, and it worked.

Later in my life, I was a butterflyer because I liked the technique. Swimming technique is fascinating and butterfly is where I really got into it. That's why this book focuses on swimming rather than running and biking; the technique is much more complicated.

I never went fully professional at swimming. Art was my profession. Swimming and athletics? Just the love of my life, what I always love to do. I like water, and much of my art includes water.

When I swim, my mind doesn't wander. I think about technique the whole time, like getting the kick just right. I enjoy the concentration. In school growing up, I liked the subjects I could get my hands on, like art, gym class, and geometry, and I enjoyed history books once I realized history could be about people, not just memorizing dates. I was never one for memorizing. Swimming is a way I can read, learn, and experience, seeing progress as I go.

When I meet someone who doesn't swim or says they don't like swimming, I don't think anything about it. Why should everybody like swimming? There are plenty of activities I don't like.

When it comes to fitness, I don't even use the "E" word— "exercise." I like a lot of athletic and active activities, but to me "exercise" is doing what's good for you even though you hate it.

Swimming, running, biking, lifting weights, travel, time with family, music, and cooking didn't exist in separate spaces for me. I was always just doing whatever I liked to do, and much of the time that was outside or being active.

The Adult Learner

So you're an adult, and you'd like to start swimming for the first time.

How do I start to swim as an adult?

You may be wondering: Should I get a coach? Read a book? Read this book? Imitate others? Each has its advantages and pitfalls. A coach who is experienced in teaching swimmers whose bones have been shaped into their sockets by instruction since childhood might not be your first choice. You need to know how you can improve or ease your particular movements, not what's best for the 20-year-old Olympic hopeful. A book might tell you one-size-fits-all information how a stroke should be swum perfectly, rather than what you can do to make progress while avoiding injury.

Imitation has drawbacks as well. When observing a stroke, we must distinguish between cause and effect. For example, the butterflyer's undulation is readily visible and new swimmers will try to imitate this with some quite funny results. In fact, that undulation is the result of timing and should not be forced. It will come naturally when the head and kick are coordinated. Likewise, in freestyle, a too-wide kick is almost always the result of excessive head movement, so any attempt to cure the kick alone will be frustrating. And snaking (over-rotating at the hips) is actually the result of not enough rolling, rather than too much.

There is another problem that we all see when watching ourselves on video, a strange disconnect between our kinesthesia and our actual movements. The video comes as a shock. We don't look how we feel, and it can be hard to believe that everyone eventually achieves a sense of relative smoothness and even elegance in the water, ourselves included. If you tell a backstroker to enter their hand 6 inches wider, they'll do one inch and feel they've done it. If you suggest that the freestyler lower their head, you might not see the difference even if it feels radically changed to the swimmer.

What works
Knowing what to look for in ourselves, carefully observing swimmers who seem very comfortable as well as reasonably fast, and asking a friend to watch you all will work very well if you have some basic information about each stroke. Keep in mind that bodies do not multitask well. That's why kids find patting their heads while making circles on their bellies a giggly challenge. Don't make more than one change at a time and not more than one change every couple of weeks.

Before starting
If you're afraid of the water, deal with that first. Read the section on fear of water. If you're gasping before you get to the end of the pool, spend six weeks building your endurance before you even think of technique or speed. Try one of the introductory plans in this book, "0 to 700" or "Building up to your first mile."

The basic idea
The basic idea of swimming is to maintain a horizontal position and use as little energy as possible to displace the most water rearward. The narrowest boat with the widest paddle is the most efficient. If your feet are dangling (perpendicular to the surface of the water), you are effectively trying to shove a body twice the thickness of yours through the water. If your stroke or kick is very wide and deep you are doing the same thing. You want to push the least amount of yourself forward by occupying the smallest amount of space. Horizontal body, shallow pull, narrow kick. At the same time, the widest paddle can be achieved by raising your elbow high at the start so that you can pull with your whole arm and not just your upper arm. Fingers closed, but not tightly, will serve you better than swimming with a wide-open fork, and a flat hand makes a larger surface than spooned.

Take your time
With a few famous exceptions, the best swimmers tend to take fewer strokes. A fast stroke turnover is only effective if each stroke efficiently presses back the maximum amount of water. It feels like pressing back, and that is only partly accurate.

It is somewhat like climbing a rope, holding your place with one hand while going forward with the other. Your concentration should be on maintaining a steady pull without losing your attention, and just letting the water slip by.

Relax

If you don't need it, don't use it. You don't need neck muscles to swim, so let them relax. Momentum will get your arm out of the water, then let your arm go quite limp until it re-enters the water. If you're not swimming very fast and don't need the extra ten percent your kick can give you, just make a little flip of your ankles to maintain the position of your body in the water. The energy you save can be directed into a vigorous pull.

Think

Whatever brings you to the pool is best achieved with your attention in the moment. Swimming is only boring if you don't think about it and don't structure your workouts or have any goals. With one exception! If you're at the pool for some necessary blank time or just to burn some calories, that's just fine.

How to do the strokes

Freestyle, aka crawl

Push off the wall, straight and narrow, arms straight in front of you and hands flat. Be patient. In a few seconds, you'll slow down. Once that happens, kick narrowly, using your hips to move your legs enough to flop your feet, letting the water bend your knees slightly.

Leave shoulder to elbow on the surface while your hand drops down until it is below your elbow. Now start pulling not very hard with your whole arm. Sense what you're doing, trying to feel the pressure of the water along your whole arm, not just your hand. Your arm now looks like a boomerang as you switch from pull to push and increase the pressure. When you think you've completed the push, go another six inches forcefully.

Let the momentum take your elbow out of the water, hand dangling behind. Your shoulder swings your arm effortlessly all the way straight in front of you. Without rushing, let the other arm begin its cycle when you're at least halfway through the recovery of the first arm. Quite a bit of variation in timing is acceptable.

Breathe in the trough that your head makes in the water so that you won't need to lift your head at all, only to turn it to the side. Maintain an even keel from your head to toe, keeping your spine

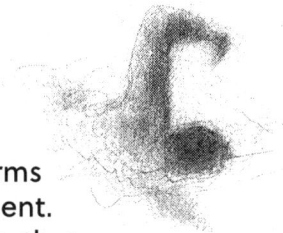

quite rigid as your torso rotates with each stroke, while your head is holding steady. Rotation is subtle. It might help you to think that your hand, when passing by your hip, is pushing your hip out of the way. Not really, of course, but that's the timing. All the movements from your head and arms travel down your body and, if not allowed to continue into a rotation, will instead cause your hips and legs to wave and snake. Have someone watch you. If you're not snaking, you're okay; otherwise you need to rotate your hips more.

Breaststroke

Seemingly so easy, the stroke of choice for relaxation is the most technically demanding of all. Timing is everything. The arms and legs are in a streamlined position, same as freestyle, and they return to that position momentarily on every stroke. More than any other stroke, the breaststroke must be watched and imitated.

The elbows stay up, again like freestyle, as the forearms sweep out and around as if inside a big salad bowl, the upper arms snapping together when the hands are coming in at the bottom of the bowl.

As the hands, together, extend forward to their beginning position, the knees bend to bring your feet very close to your butt and pointed out. While still extending your arms, your legs imitate your armstroke. They circle out, around, and snap back and together. Hold it for a second in the glide position. Breathing takes place when your arms, snapping together under your chin, push water up, raising your chin. Head goes back down as arms go forward.

Backstroke

The stroke of choice for beginners because you can breathe whenever and however you want, although you'll likely form a pattern and stick to it without thinking about it.

As with the other strokes, push off the wall streamlined and underwater. When you surface for your first breath and armstroke, look for your hip and keep the left one in sight while you stroke with your right arm, then the right hip with the left arm. This means that your head will not be thrown back. It will stay in the same position, up, as your body turns on its axis. Even the kick will turn left and right. This body roll is much more pronounced than with freestyle. As in freestyle, your hand passing the hip is the time to begin the rotation.

With your body on its side (but nose up!) your arm can much more easily sink, bend at the elbow, pull and push, and exit thumb first. With this roll, you don't have to reach behind your back to get your arm and hand in the water; your body will be on its side, so you are stroking more comfortably because your side is well down in the water and your arm is naturally in the correct position.

Butterfly

Sure. Why not. It's not that big a deal. The only thing that makes it so strenuous is the awkwardness of breathing when both arms are out of the water. You have to kick very hard to get your whole upper body in a position that allows your mouth to do you the favor of taking in air instead of water. Simple solution: Don't breathe. That's not as totally impractical as it seems. In a race, the flyer may take 0 to 1 breath in the first 25 yards and 1 or 2 coming back. As a learner, you can practice 4 or 5 strokes without breathing and then just stand up if it's shallow or continue with another stroke until the end of the pool. Rest and start again.

To start, we'll not only do without air, we won't bother with arms either. First: Arms at side, feet together, dive your head down, stand up; over and over and over. Next: Arms at side, dive head down, and when you feel your legs surface, kick them forcefully down and raise your head. Now stand up and repeat many times. Next: Do the same thing, but after your head comes up, kick and dive again without standing. You can take a little gasp when your head rises. Gradually, make the dive more shallow until you are just undulating without needing to stand. When that becomes almost easy, try going across the pool kicking your head down and kicking your head up, breathing whenever you like. When you can do that, you've got the hard part down pat.

One would think that swimming butterfly with only one arm is a special kind of aquatic torture, but it's actually easy for the same reason two arms is hard: breathing. So, next: Add only one arm to the kicking. The arm recovers when your head is up and enters immediately after your head enters. When you progress to two arms, it will feel easier at first for your arms to be straight out to the sides during recovery. As you get more familiar with the stroke, your arms will be less straight, like in freestyle.

All four strokes

There's a nice sense of accomplishment in being able to swim all four strokes. Put them together in the order of Fly, Back, Breast, Free, and you'll have the Individual Medley, which is raced at distances from 100 to 400 yards or meters.

Fear of Swimming and Water

Ideally, a baby is bathed lovingly, taken to the beach early, played with in the water, and almost learns to swim on their own before they ever begin lessons. Many are introduced to the water later, however, and the fear is overwhelming. Often, the child or adult is first told to swim on their back to avoid confronting their fear. What could be worse! If you were worried about a monster in your house, you wouldn't enter backward.

For a child, teach them to play in and with the water. Eyes open under water, just sit and look around, look at you, touch, look at others, move under water, go between your legs. When they become more confident, have them jump off your shoulders. Hold their hands and twirl them around, asking if you should let go. The idea is that water is fun, more forgiving than land, and its mysteries are joyful rather than fearful. Once they learn to play in it, learning to swim will be a welcome tool to further enjoy the water.

For an adult, wear comfortable goggles. Spend time adjusting them so they don't leak. Depending on your fear level, you might start by just visiting the pool, putting your feet in, wading in a nearby body of water, running your face under the shower water, and practicing going under the water to hold your breath or blow some bubbles (by breathing out through your nose) before coming back up. Bring a friend and try some playing like described above. You might prefer to step down into the pool rather than jump in.

Adults often fear that they will not be able to float while swimming. When you're ready, sit at the bottom of the shallow end of the pool. This is not easy because your body wants to float even if you think you can't. Look around at the other swimmers under water. Spend a whole session doing nothing else but sitting and looking. Next time, try to move around under water, staying close to the bottom. Do not try to float. Do not lie on your back. Bring someone with you, if possible.

As you move around under water, you'll notice that it's difficult to stay down. Now, you may let yourself rise. With the slightest movement of your unbent legs and floppy feet, you will remain on the surface, face down. When you feel comfortable in the water and have begun to take a few lessons, go to an open body of water and do the same thing, sitting at the bottom and looking around. Now, there will be a more interesting view, perhaps some plants, a few fish, or even shells. It's truly fascinating. No wonder so many people love the water.

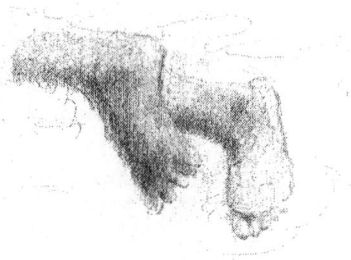

Glossary

Competitive strokes and events

These are the types of swimming strokes and events that people compete in. Swimmers with disabilities use strokes adapted for their physiology.

Butterfly, also called fly	Face down. Double arm (meaning arms move simultaneously) and double kick with body undulation and straight arm recovery.
Backstroke, also called back crawl	Face up. Alternating arms, alternating kick. The body has a pronounced roll on each arm pull.
Breaststroke	Face down. Double arms, double kick. Underwater recovery. A modified frog kick, also called a whip kick.
Freestyle, also called crawl	Face down. Alternating arms, alternating kick. Breathing to the side. This is a standard stroke used by everyone.
Medley Relay	Four swimmers compete doing one each of the above, in that order.
Individual Medley, or IM	An individual person racing fly, backstroke, breaststroke, and freestyle, in that order.

Recreational strokes

Includes all of the strokes above of course, in addition to the below.

Sidestroke	Completely on one side, one arm does upper half stroke, the other does the lower, with a scissor kick
Trudgen Crawl	Face down. Same as freestyle, but with a scissor kick.

Elementary Backstroke	Face up. Double arm underwater, like breaststroke except only up to the shoulder. Frog kick.
Underwater swimming	Same as breaststroke, but continue the stroke all the way back and don't come up.
Dog Paddle	You know what this is. It can be fun to do during cool down.

Workout terms

Here are some of the terms you'll find in the workouts in this book.

SKPS	Swim Kick Pull Swim. For example, for a 4x200 SKPS, you would swim 50, kick 50 with a kick board, pull 50 with a pull buoy, and swim 50, then rest for a specified time and repeat three more times to add up to 4x200.
Kick	Usually with a board stretched out in front of you.
Pull	Plastic foam pull buoy between legs to concentrate on the pull without kicking.
Interval	Start each section at a particular time as specified in the workout. The rest time will vary based on how fast you swim.
Repeat	Rest for a specified length of time. For example, swim ten times 50 yards, rest 15 seconds between each swim.
Go on	Denotes when you start swimming, regardless of how long you took to swim. For example, you might "go on 75," meaning to start a set of swimming every 75 seconds regardless of how long the swim takes.

DPS (Distance per stroke)	The number of yards one armstroke takes you. In a workout, sometimes refers to counting strokes to increase the DPS or reduce the number of strokes it takes to go a given distance.
SC (Stroke cycle)	The completion of both arms of a stroke.
Fartlek	A Swedish term meaning "speed play," where you add varying speeds during a continuous swim, usually based on individual feeling.
Set	A related group of swims, like multiple bites of a single course in a menu. For example, 4x200.
Warmup (WU)	A short swim or series of swims to raise your heart rate, loosen up, and get your body ready for a workout.
Warmdown/Cooldown/ Swim-down	A short swim to help the body relax, get ready to end the workout, and avoid soreness.
Taper	Decreasing workouts during the days or weeks leading up to a competition or performance.

Common types of sets

The workouts in this book will include several popular structures, introduced below. A set will include a number of yards, e.g. 300; or, a number of times to do a number of yards, e.g. 10x200.

Ladder	Increase or decrease the yardage as you go. For example, 100, 200, 300, 400.
Pyramid	Increase and then decrease the yardage. For example, 100, 200, 300, 200, 100.
Straight	A distance swum without stopping. For example, 500, 400.
Broken	A distance divided into shorter swims. For example, 10x50.

Alternating straight/ broken	Switching between straight and broken distances. For example, 500, 10x50, 400, 8x50.
Descending	Decreasing either the number of strokes or the time. For example, you could swim 50 yards while counting strokes. Then, you could swim the same speed with fewer strokes, or swim 2 seconds faster with fewer strokes.

Section 2: Building a Base

I remember the first day I went to the pool when I started swimming again around age 50. Someone else was coming out of the pool as I was going in. She looked a little bit old, a little bit dilapidated. She didn't look like she was nearly as fast as me, but she swam a straight mile and I thought, oh my gosh, if she can do that, then so can I. So, my very first day I got in the pool, I swam a mile. When I was done, I practically crawled out of the pool. There was nothing left of me!

This section provides a plan for how you can get from swimming not at all to being able to swim 700 yards at once, and how you can get from 700 to a mile. This will set the foundation for you to enjoy yourself from there, including adding workouts like the ones that appear later in this book.

If swimming 100 yards is not yet possible, then start with the Zero to 700. Otherwise, go ahead and try the Zero to 1650 (mile) plan.

Zero to 700
An easy preamble to the 0-1650 plan

It has been brought to my attention that my plan for swimming Zero to One Mile in six weeks does not in fact start from zero, but rather 700 yards or meters. It begins with 100-yard repetitions (reps) plus shorter distances that equal 700. If you already run or bicycle or do other aerobic exercise, swimming 100 yards several times may be no sweat. But if you're coming straight from the couch to the pool, some preparation that begins at true zero would be useful.

Like a scar forms in response to a wound, like a muscle enlarges to meet new demands, so does our ability to absorb oxygen. If we methodically increase our need, our body kindly responds. The amount of discomfort should be small. It is necessary to pant a bit at the end of each effort and to not fully recover (i.e. your breathing and heart rate won't fully return to resting) before beginning another part of the workout.

Start with three days per week:

First swim day
Start walking in the pool. Then try running. If the pool supplies belts for water running, use one. If not, that's fine. After 5 or 10 minutes of water walking/running, put on a cap and goggles. The cap goes first so that goggles will not pull at your hair. Adjust the goggles. Sit at the bottom of the pool to reassure yourself they will not leak. Swim any stroke on your front or side at all, disregarding technique. As soon as you feel like stopping, flop over and do any kind of backstroke. When you tire, switch to another stroke, such as sidestroke, if possible still without stopping. If you do stop, keep the rest short until you are breathing somewhat more easily, but are

not fully recovered. You must experience some discomfort because that is how you tell that bubble wrap to increase its surface area and those annoyed little organelles to multiply. The effect takes place quickly, and easier recovery days in between workout days are necessary for the growth to occur.

Second and third swim days
Whatever you found most enjoyable may be continued. Increase the total distance you're covering by using any stroke that makes it possible to continue forward motion. A kickboard is sufficiently unpleasant to be useful, but stay away from pull-buoys. Your quads are big muscles that demand a lot of oxygen, and if you don't use them at all because of the pull-buoy flotation, you lose out on a lot of progress that you could be triggering your body to make.

Second week
Increase the amount of freestyle, but still change strokes rather than stop. Once you can swim two 25-yard (or meter) laps, rest for a maximum of 12 breaths, and repeat this 3 more times (400 yards total), then you can go on to the following simple workout:

- » 100 any stroke to warm up
- » 3 x 100 (12 breaths in between each 100 to rest)
- » 3 x 75 (10 breaths rest)
- » 3 x 25 (6 breaths rest)

Achieving the goal
Within a few weeks, you will likely be ready for the Zero to One Mile program, which appears next in this book.

Will it get easier?
Now, about this breathing and discomfort business. At this stage, you don't need gasping or 100% effort. Will there come a day when you are completely relaxed and breathing gently and easily throughout the swim? Not really, if you're continuing to get stronger and faster. The wish to be a bit better, which in aerobic sports like swimming and running means faster, remains with us. As we improve, most of us strive harder and continue to raise our heart rates, so there is always a bit of panting. It feels good! And most of us find that we are more productive during the rest of the day as a result of working out.

Zero to 1650
Swimming a mile in 6 weeks

Young or old, fit or not, six weeks seems to be the most common length of time it takes to become able to swim a mile without stopping for rest. It requires swimming three times per week and the willingness to be somewhat uncomfortable while stretching your aerobic capability. The feeling of not having adequate rest is necessary to improve. I expect that the number of breaths you take before continuing will not seem enough, and I also promise you'll be surprised that you are able to continue much more easily than you imagined.

I gave a lot of thought to the 0 to 1650 plan. I looked into the mechanics and physiology to add medical information to my own judgement, to figure out how it could be done—and it worked for everybody. It's still used by people of all ages across the world, and it can work for you as well.

The Zero to 1650 plan

Using this plan:

» Each workout is done three times per week.

» If your pool is 50 yards/meters, use 2x50 instead of 4x25.

Week	Distances (yards or meters)	Number of breaths to rest between efforts within each set
1	4 x 100 4 x 50 4 x 25 = 700	12 8 4
2	200 4 x 100 4 x 50 4 x 25 = 900	12 10 6 4
3	400 200 4 x 100 4 x 50 = 1200	12 10 8 4
4	600 300 4 x100 4 x 50 = 1500	10 8 6 4
5	1000 4 x 100 4 x 50 = 1600	8 4 4
6 (days 1 & 2)	1200 3 x 100 3 x 50	8 4 4
6 (day 3)	1650 yards or 1500 meters straight	No breaks. Congratulations!

A few hints

If you think you're really too breathless just to get to the end of the pool, let your legs drag. The quads, being so big, take a disproportionate amount of oxygen. Any muscle will, of course, require more oxygen when in use than when relaxed, so if you don't need to use the muscle, don't. Even relaxing your neck will help make the swim easier, or relaxing your arms while recovering during the stroke. Speed is not your aim during these six weeks, nor is the perfect stroke. These come later, or they may not come at all if your intention is just to enjoy the water, to relax, or to get some pleasant movement.

If you can't do the whole distance via freestyle (crawl), you may wonder if you can switch up your stroke. I'm often asked if changing strokes defeats the purpose of the whole idea. Of course not. Also, once you build stamina and go on to other workouts, other strokes are part of the scheme. They add to your skills and provide enjoyable variety. After you've gone the distance any way you can, you can build your stamina by eliminating the resting strokes, but when you're first starting out you can get the distance by any and all means.

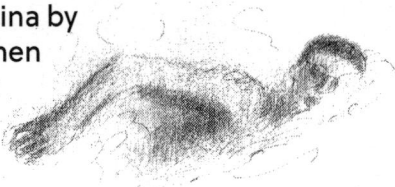

A few words about technique up to your first mile

It is said by many that technique is everything, yet I've said very little here about it. I've noticed that most of the big problems of a beginner disappear on their own by the time they can swim a straight mile.

Examples: Holding the head too high is the most common problem. As you become more comfortable, gravity kindly assists you and it goes down without attention. A stable head invariably transfers to a narrower kick, so the second most common problem— too much kicking—disappears on its own. When you kick too much, you use too much oxygen and some of the motion goes against the water instead of propelling you forward. Body position is very important as well because every part of your body that takes up unneeded space in the water will slow you down.

After these first 6 weeks, however, is technique really everything as you continue to build strength? Yes. Technique means nothing more than making the stroke simpler and using less energy, so that your effort is channeled directly into propelling you forward. I recommend that you not tie yourself up in knots and get discouraged by technical concerns in the beginning. You're here to enjoy some movement, not go to the Olympics. Once you're ready, check out the sections of this book about technique and additional swim skills.

Section 3: Transitioning To Workouts

You followed the Zero to 1650 plan and now after 6 weeks you can swim a straight mile just a little bit slower than the slowest person in the pool. Nice work! While that's good enough, you also want to enjoy it, and maybe continue making progress, even if you have no interest in racing. So, now what?

It's time to do workouts. Structured swims allow us to improve and grow in ways beyond how we might from casually swimming. And pure laps become same-old very quickly. This section will offer you some ways to add structured workouts to your routine.

Intervals are my favorite type of workout because they're constructed in a way that is pleasant; you feel like you've accomplished something. You can go faster or slower, and you can do a variety of things rather than just get in and stay wet for a half hour. I did speed workouts every week.

For me, the outcome of winning wasn't my primary goal. So swimming workouts were about the activity itself; swimming workouts are an activity I like to do. Part of that activity is doing my best, and part of doing my best is being better than everyone else! So participating in races included competing and winning, not just being there. Since the workouts were both a means to a competitive end and a pleasure in themselves, when I decided to stop competing at age 80 after a fall impacted my training, it wasn't hard to cope with because stopping competing didn't mean I had to stop training. I hope that you, too, will find pleasure in pushing yourself and building strength through workouts.

Learning the mechanics and technique of swimming has captured my attention for decades. This section includes information to develop your repertoire of techniques and skills. While none of these are required for the workouts in this book, you may find that you, too, enjoy the technique involved or add them in for some spice.

Many workouts for newer swimmers begin with a warm-up, then sets of intervals and/or repeats, followed by practicing new strokes and drills. The warm-up helps your muscles get going and helps your cardiovascular system get ready to take in and use more oxygen to fuel your workout.

Swimming for Fitness: A Basic Plan

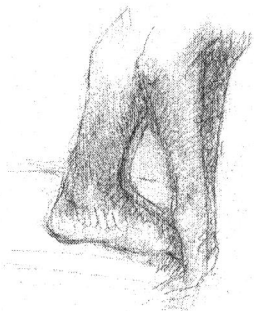

Assuming you want to swim for one hour 3 times per week, it's probably a good idea to continue the one mile on session one out of three, and then switch it up the other two sessions. For maximum fitness benefits, it helps to exercise at different speeds to vary and occasionally raise your heart rate. Using different strokes strengthens different muscles and keeps you interested.

Here's a basic plan you can use and adapt each week.

Day One, each week: Distance. Swim for as long as you know it takes you to go one mile. If you have extra time left in the hour, do whatever other strokes you already know.

Day Two: Speed. Swim 15 minutes, kick 10 minutes, swim as fast as you can 5 minutes. Swim any other stroke you know 10 minutes. Swim the other stroke 1 length as fast as you can. Rest and repeat 4 times. Run in the water for 10 minutes.

Day Three: Drill/Skills: Learn something new. Swim 15 minutes. Choose a stroke you don't know and swim several lengths. Kick the new stroke 5 minutes. Swim freestyle 10 minutes. Swim with one arm, changing arms after one length. Try breathing on your non-natural side. Swim with fists instead of flat hands. Swim any stroke 5 minutes.

Some additional ways to spice things up:
» Bring a friend or two to the pool.
» Become familiar with the pace clock.
» Try some drills.

» Use toys like the pull buoy, kickboard, and fins (bring your own or use the ones at the pool), though don't overuse them. The pull buoy, for example, can easily become a crutch, especially for people with ankles that are inflexible from age or from cycling strength.

» Base the quantities and lengths in your workout on one number to make it easier to remember if you don't want to write it down. E.g. 5x25, 5x50, 500.

Objective for Swimming Workouts

Most swim training is based on any of three primary objectives: Go long. Go easy. Go fast.

Go long

Take a look at the Zero to 1650 chapter of this book for a detailed plan for how to build distance. If you are just beginning, there are essentially two ways to increase your distance.

First way: Do a mile from day one, changing your stroke to anything easy, even sidestroke and elementary backstroke, whenever necessary. After a week, restrict the non-freestyle to something like every fourth lap, later to every eighth lap, until you've eliminated non-freestyle altogether.

Second way: Using no alternative strokes, swim shorter distances, strictly limiting rest time to ten breaths, gradually increasing the yardage. Both methods should take about six weeks until you are able to do the whole mile non-stop, all freestyle.

Go easy

This is a matter of technique which primarily consists of: Do not get in your own way. What does that mean? Mostly a series of Do Nots. Do Not place or move any part of your body in such a way as to interfere with your forward progress. Sounds obvious, doesn't it? Here are some examples:

» Do not allow your kick to be very deep or extend beyond the width of your body.
» Keep your arms within the invisible narrow tube in which you are swimming.
» Move your head as little as possible, in a line with your torso.
» Do not tense up with excessive concern for your technique.

The swim training theory may have little to do with what is best for you because it changes frequently and is often based on observing whoever won recent Olympic swims. You can improve your own methods by imitating those whose swimming you think seems both effortless and fast, and you can do drills at least once per week.

Regarding drills: Check out the drills chapter of this book, right after this one, and do drills weekly. It is also a good idea to count your strokes frequently and reduce them if you can do so without slowing down. This being said, although the best swimmers often have very low stroke counts, some fast world class swimmers, such as Janet Evans, do not. Do what works for you.

Go fast

There is only one way to increase your speed. You must break the distance into smaller segments that can be swum faster than your race distance pace. This is the meat and potatoes (or Powerbar and Gu) of all swim training. These are intervals. Rests may be very short, medium, or quite long. Do all three. Here are a few examples of common styles of intervals:

Broken 100s
4x25 meters on :30. Repeat this 4 times with 30 seconds between each set of 4.
= 500

Ladder
400, 4x100; 300, 4x75; 200, 4x50; 100, 4x25
= 2000

Pyramid
2x50 on :60, 2x100 on 2:00, 2x150 on 3:00, 2x200 on 4:00, and back down
= 1600

Ladder
200, 2x175, 3x150, 4x125, 5x100, 6x75, 7x50, 8x25
= 3000

Race distance ÷ 100
If, for example, you plan to do a half Ironman, swim 20X100 with very short rests.

Race distance ÷ 10

If, for example, you plan to swim an Ironman, go 10x400 with short rests.

Putting it together

If you are swimming three times per week, concentrate on distance one day, speed another, and drills/skills another, feeling free to vary the content and order. Variations, using different strokes and employing swim toys such as kickboard, pull buoy, and fins, will make it easier and more pleasant to increase the length of your workout. Check out the workouts in this book for more examples.

Drills

The following drills will help you practice your technique for the four main competition strokes.

Butterfly
» No arms, hands at your sides. Think: Kick head down, kick head up. Don't rush the kick. It begins at the chest and unfurls quite slowly with a snap of the ankles, like cracking a whip. If your timing is good on the whole stroke, this will be very easy. If it's difficult to do, your timing is likely off. Within a fraction of a second, the sequence of entry is head, hands, feet. The second kick is half way through the stroke.
» One arm strokes, the other remains forward, breathe to side or forward. Change arms at wall.
» Lots of kicking, with and without board, with and without fins, because propulsion is easily 30% from kick.

Backstroke
» Roll totally onto your side, even kicking sideways. One arm straight above you in water, the other straight toward your feet. Take one stroke, roll to other side with NO twisting. Take one stroke with other arm. Kick at 6 to 9 times and switch again.

Breaststroke
» Swim with dolphin (butterfly) kick to introduce undulation into the stroke.
» Touch your heels to get your full kick.
» Experiment breathing immediately and at the last moment.
» Kick twice, pull once for a length; then kick once and pull twice.

Freestyle

» One arm: Swim with one arm, changing which arm at wall.

» Catch-up: Hand touches outstretched hand before you pull.

» Fist swimming: Get a feel for the work your whole arm does on the water, without the use of your hands.

» Ripple: Skim your fingers across the water, directly below your elbow, during recovery while your elbow is held high directly above your hand.

» Hypoxic swim: Reduce number of breaths. Easier with a pull-buoy. Numbers listed in a workout denote the ratio of the number of breath to strokes ratio. For example, 1/4 is one breath per four strokes.

» Underwater recovery: Slide hand forward close to torso.

» Hesitation: Leave your hand out of the water behind you for a second before beginning recovery

» Exaggerated roll: stay on side, but facing forward for several kicks.

» Tarzan: Swim with your head up, a handy ability for triathlons and other open-water swims.

To Kick or Not to Kick

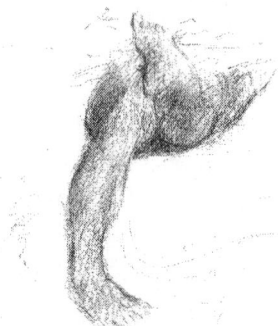

To kick or not to kick? A bicyclist might ask this question, saying that their legs are so muscular they sink. Other swimmers ask why they go backward when they use a kickboard. Many want to know how they can correct wiggling from side to side. "What is the timing of the kick, and how many kicks per stroke?" is usually a single question.

The freestyle kick is overrated

Although backstrokers, butterflyers, and especially breaststrokers can get 30 to 50% of their power from the kick, the greatest freestylers achieve only 10%. That marginal improvement costs a great deal of oxygen, especially with an inefficient kick, and this oxygen would be better spent by arms. But then, won't your legs sink? That is a matter of body position. Arch your back, being careful to keep your head down, and your legs will rise.

Coordinating

Your body kindly coordinates itself without needing you to micromanage. When you walk, you don't have to think "left leg forward and left arm back." Your legs not only manage on their own, they compensate for your faults. When I see a wide kick, perhaps fishtailing, or too low, I look first at the swimmer's head. Almost certainly it is too high and swinging sideways with each breath. By the time that movement reaches the feet, it's a serious drag.

What to do

Swim without kicking at first, until your legs learn the rhythm of your arms and head. Have someone look at you to see if your leg position is narrow, neat, and tidy. If not, watch your head and look for crossover arm strokes. Once you've straightened out your stroke, experiment with your rhythm: How many kicks per stroke and whether you place extra emphasis every few kicks. If you breathe bilaterally (on both sides), this will be another rhythm. They are all okay. They all serve the purpose of keeping you on keel.

Watch out behind me!

It's not the kickboard's fault. If you move backward when you kick, it is because you are pushing water forward. How can that be? Bent knees can do it and bent ankles always will. Use your hips to make your loose feet flop around like rag dolls. Make sure you're kicking from your hips rather than your knees by keeping your legs straight. The only movement of the knees should be a side effect of water on very relaxed legs. Use your hips and feet. Nothing else. Vigorous hip action drives floppy feet. This can be very difficult for bicyclists whose feet work like pistons. It can be difficult for cyclists and runners not to use their legs vigorously. With practice, you will learn this new style of using your legs and hips.

Flip Turns

Here are a few suggestions for someone who has never tried flip turns. They are not rules written in stone and are not meant for experienced turners.

Do exhale through your nose forcefully as you rotate.
Don't hold your breath going into the turn.

Do practice your turns in open water, far from the wall.
Don't complicate the task by trying to place your feet on the wall.

Do come up completely on your back while you are learning.
Don't try to twist into a freestyle position.

Do maintain speed. Your momentum will make the turn easier.
Don't slow down before you flip.

Do turn your hands from palms facing up to palms facing the bottom of the pool. When both your arms are at your side and you have not yet swung your legs over yourself, your arms are already in the correct position facing the direction you want to go.
Don't flail your arms everywhere after you've turned over. This is a major problem for almost all new flippers because the correct arm position feels counter-intuitive.

The flip turn, simplified
Swim fast. Simultaneously and quickly do the following: Tuck your chin to your chest while pulling your outstretched arm to your side (your other arm is at your other side already), and make a little dolphin kick. Be patient and don't do anything else until you are

folded in two with legs quite straight and eyes looking up to the surface of the water. Then, turn your palms down and press on them while bending your legs. With that, your turn is complete. Don't forget to leave your arms alone. It's your hips that leave your hands, not the other way around.

After a week or so you can try the wall. You will certainly be too far away from it, so ask someone to tell you how much closer you can get. If you do ten turns after every practice, you can expect to do reliable flips in about four weeks.

Section 4: Swim Workouts

This section includes 5 introductory workouts that are great for newer swimmers, 10 quick lunchtime workouts, and a collection of 51 comprehensive, scaleable swim workouts. They have been the core of my swimming website for years, and after over 12 million visits to my website, it's time for them to be in print! I hope you find them interesting to read and useful for your swimming practice.

Using the workouts
» All distances listed are in yards. You can use meters or adjust to your needs.
» Check out the drills page earlier in this book to choose what to add when workouts suggest drills.
» Look at the glossary page for explanations of terms used.
» The stroke or the section of the workout is in **bold** (e.g. Free, Fly, warmup, pyramid).
» The style of moving is <u>underlined</u> (swim, pull, kick, drills).

Five Introductory Swim Workouts

Here are some workouts to get you started. Each is 2,000 yards or meters. Each workout demonstrates a common structure for a swim workout.

Intro Workout 1: Ladder	
Warm-up Free Swim Count strokes, try to take fewer.	500
Ladder Choice of stroke Swim	5x100 rest 20 sec 5x75 rest 15 sec 5x50 rest 10 sec 5x25 rest 5 sec
Backstroke SKDS Big hip roll	5x50

Intro Workout 2: Pyramid	
Warm-up Freestyle <u>Swim</u> with pronounced finish past hip	400
Pyramid Choice of stroke <u>Swim</u> Rest 15 sec after each rep	4x50 3x100 200 3x100 4x50
Breaststroke <u>Drills, swim, pull, kick</u>	400

Intro Workout 3: Descending sets	
Warm-up Free <u>Swim</u> bilateral breathing	300
Descending sets Choice of stroke <u>Swim</u>	3(4x75): Each 75 is 2 sec faster. Rest 15 sec Repeat 3 times.
Butterfly <u>Drills, kick</u> e.g. Hands at side, kick head down, kick head up. <u>Swim</u> <u>Drill</u> 1-arm swim	300 4x25 100

Intro Workout 4: Sprints & IM	
Warm-up Freestyle <u>Swim</u> think about high elbow	400
Sprints Choice of stroke <u>Swim</u> <u>Kick</u> short fins if you have them <u>Pull</u> very easy	4x25 rest 5 sec 4x25 rest 10 sec 4x25 rest 15 sec 100 very hard! 400 400
Individual Medley (IM) <u>SPKS</u>	4x100

Intro Workout 5: IM	
Warm-up Freestyle <u>Swim</u> Try slightly different paths for pull	500
Individual Medley (IM) <u>Swim</u>	5x100 favorite stroke 5x75 almost favorite 5x50 not so favorite 5x25 really don't like
Worst stroke <u>Drills</u>	250

10 Lunchtime Swim Workouts

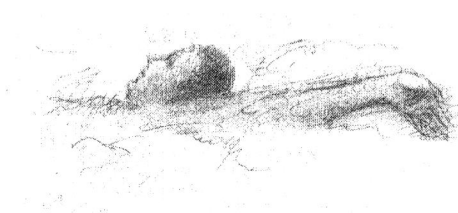

It's going to take more than an hour to get to the pool, change, shower, and change again unless your workplace includes a swimming hole. Even then, there likely isn't time for some of the details that are standard in a swim workout: long warm-ups, lots of attention to technique, plenty of drills, and a long warmdown. Assuming you have under an hour to change clothes, swim, and run through the shower, you might be able to get through these basic swims. If you're sore the next day, though, add a little warmdown. Even a hundred yards will help.

Lunch Workout 1: Alternating Free & IM	
Free	200
IM+free, up the lane stroke, return free	2x175
Free <u>swim, kick, pull</u>	3x150
IM add 25 stroke to end (rotate)	4x125
Free <u>drill</u> up the lane, <u>swim</u> back	5x100
45 minutes intermediate	2000

Lunch Workout 2: IM Technique + free	
Free	500
Fly <u>swim, kick</u> fast	2x50
Free pattern:	3x150
1 pay attention to first third of pull	
2 think of elbow pushing middle of pull	
3 push hard at end of pull	
Backstroke <u>swim, kick</u> fast	
Free pattern	2x50
Breaststroke <u>swim, kick</u> fast	3x50
Free pattern	2x50
Free very fast	3x50
Free pattern	2x50
	3x50
45 minutes beginner-intermediate	1500

Lunch Workout 3: Free with toys, IM swim	
Free	400
IM If you can't swim 100 fly, do what you can, e.g. one-arm	4x100
Free <u>pull</u> easy, with pull buoy	300
IM	4x75
Free <u>kick</u>	200
IM <u>swim</u>	4x50
Free, <u>drill</u> e.g. catch-up	100
IM <u>swim</u> very hard	4x25
60 minutes intermediate 40 minutes advanced	2000

Lunch Workout 4: Really short lunch break	
Free	
<u>Swim</u>	600
<u>Swim</u>	6x75, rest 15 sec
<u>Kick</u> or <u>pull</u>	6x50
<u>Swim</u> hard, rest 5 sec	6x25
30 minutes, or longer with long rests	1500

Lunch Workout 5: Favorite and not favorite strokes	
Free	400
Favorite stroke <u>swim</u>	8x50
Choice <u>kick</u>	300
Like a lot stroke <u>swim</u>	6x50
Choice <u>pull</u>	200
Don't like stroke <u>swim</u>	4x50
Choice <u>drill</u>	100
Really hate stroke <u>swim</u>	2x50
50 minutes beginner-intermediate	2000

Lunch Workout 6: Pyramid A	
Choice	300
<u>Swim</u> 50 each:	
Fly, Free, Back, Free, Breast, Free	6x50
Swim Each 25 of the 100:	3x100
1 Fly Free Free Fly	
2 Bk Free Free Bk	
3 Br Free Free Br	
IM kick	300
<u>Swim</u> Each 25 of the 100:	3x100
1 Free Fly Free Fly,	
2 Free Bk Free Bk	
3 Free Br Free Br	
IM, Free <u>Drills</u>	6x50
50 minutes beginner	1800

Lunch Workout 7: Pyramid B	
Choice or **Free**	
<u>Swim</u>	4x50
Short rests, maybe 10 seconds.	3x100
	2x150
	1x200
	2x150
	3x100
	4x50
50 minutes if rests are short	1800

Lunch Workout 8: Bare bones basic	
One mile straight swim. Every 4th lap, either change stroke or speed up for 50 yards	1650 (1760 land mile or 1650 swimmer's mile/1500 meters)
30 minutes is considered a respectable time	1650

Lunch Workout 9: Hardcore & short	
Free	400
IM	200
Fly rest is about half length of swim	4x25
Back	4x25
Breast	4x25
Free	4x25
IM drills	200
Free kick	200
30 minutes	1400

Lunch Workout 10: A learning experience	
Choose a stroke you want to learn or the stroke you struggle with most. Let me guess: Fly. This workout will solve that. **Stroke**	
Swim easy	300
Kick no board, arms at sides	3x100
Swim one-arm	3x75
Pull one length learning stroke, return choice	3x50
Swim	3x25
Kick, Drill, Pull, Swim one length each, where Swim is a stroke that's easy for you.	350
40 minutes. Learning takes more time.	1400

51 Swim Workouts

In this set of 51 workouts, the first 12 are a little easier than the final 38. This said, your pace and style of conducting each workout is your own and can be as hard as you make it. Most of the workouts contain two options for the total distance.

Workout I: Straight Freestyle + Broken Choice		
	3200	2400
Warm-up Drills 1-arm Fly, Breast with fly kick, catch-up free, etc	400	200
Freestyle + stroke Swim Free Swim Favorite stroke Kick Free Swim 2nd favorite stroke Pull Free Swim 3rd favorite Swim Free Swim least liked stroke	20 sec rests 400 4x100 300 6x75 200 8x50 100 10x25	 400 4x100 300 4x75 200 4x50 100 4x25
IM Swim	200	100
Swim-down Swim Choice	200	100

Workout 2: Free 1650 pyramid, then Backstroke		
	3000	**2000**
Warm-up Choice Swim	500	300
Freestyle Swim Pyramid	2x50 on :45 2x100 on 1:30 2x150 on 2:15 2x200 on 3:00 2x150 on 2:15 2x100 on 1:30 2x50 on :45	2x50 on :60 2x100 on 2:00 2x150 on 3:00 1x200 on 4:00 2x150 on 3:00 2x100 on 2:00 2x50 on :60
Backstroke Kick & Swim: 1 length kick no board 1 length swim	300	200
IM Swim	300	100
Swim-down Choice Pull hypoxic	300	100

Workout 3: 1650 Free ladder, then IM 25s		
	3200	**2400**
Warm-up Reverse IM Drills	400	200
Freestyle Swim Ladder Kick	1650 11 lengths, 10, 9, ... 1 10 sec rest 250	1650 11 lengths, 10, 9, ... 1 15 sec rest 150
IM Drill Relaxed recovery Swim	100 24x25 (6 of each stroke)	100 8x25 (2 of each stroke)
Swim-down Choice Swim	200	100

Workout 4: Mostly Freestyle		
	3300	2100
Warm-up Reverse IM Drills	300	200
Freestyle Swim Kick Swim Pull Swim	300 6x50 on:45 or :50 300 6x50 on:40 or :45 300 6x50 on:35 or :40	200 6x50 on :60 200 6x50 on :55 200 6x50 on :50
Breaststroke Kick	200	200
IM Swim	400	200
Choice Swim Choice	8x25	4x25
Swim-down Choice Swim long strokes	200	100

Workout 5: Freestyle, Choice, and IM		
	3400	**2500**
Warm-up Swim	400	300
Free + Choice Kick Pull Swim	200 12x25 10 sec rest 200 12x50 rest as needed 200 12x75 rest as needed	200 8x25 15 sec rest 200 8x50 on :75 or less 200 8x75 on :75 or less
IM Drills Swim Kick	200 100 200	100 100 100
Swim-down Free Drill: Hold position on each side for several kicks per stroke	200	100

Workout 6: Straight IMs + broken strokes		
	3000	2100
Warm-up Swim Choice Drills Back: Dolphin kick to flags, 1 arm, stroke kick on side, other arm.	200 2x100	200 4x25
IM + Stroke Swim IM Free IM Breast IM Back IM Fly	400 4x100 300 4x75 200 4x50 100 4x25	100 4x100 100 4x75 100 4x50 100 4x25
Choice Kick	200 8x25	200 8x25
Swim-down Free Drill Count strokes & reduce the number	100	100

Workout 7: Straight Freestyle and broken Choice		
	3000	**2500**
Warm-up Swim, Drills Choice	400	200
Freestyle + Choice Swim		
Free	400	400
Favorite stroke	4x100	4x100
Free	300	300
2nd favorite	4x75	4x75
Free	200	200
3rd favorite	4x50	4x50
Free	100	100
The stroke you really hate	4x25	4x25
Kick Free, kick silently under water	200	100
Choice	8x50	4x25
Swim-down Choice Pull	200	100

Workout 8: All Freestyle 25s to 500		
	3500	2100
Warm-up Choice Swim	500	300
Freestyle Swim Pull hypoxic 1/4 or 1/5 Kick	10x50 on :45 10x100 on 1:30 1x500 10x25 on :30 250 250 10x25 on :35	6x50 on :60 6x100 on1:30 1x300 6x25 on :40 1x150 1x150 6x25 on :45
Swim-down Choice Pull	100	100

Workout 9: Freestyle Pyramid		
	3400	2300
Warm-up Free Drills	200	200
Choice (not Free) SKPS	4x200	4x100
Free Swim pyramid	4x50 on :45 3x100 on 1:30 2x150 on 2:15 1x200 on 3: 2x150 on 2:15 3x100 on 1:30 4x50 on :45	4x50 on :60 3x100 on 2:00 2x150 on 3: 1x200 on 4: 2x150 on 3:00 3x100 on 2:00 4x50 on :60
Kick Free	400	400
Swim-down Choice Swim	200	100

Workout 10: Freestyle ladder + Choice set		
	3400	**2400**
Warm-up Free <u>Swim, Kick, Drill</u> 50 each	3x150 rest 15 sec between 150s	2x150, rest 20 sec between 150s
Free <u>Swim</u>	400 2x200 rest 20 sec 4x100 rest 15 sec 8x50 rest 10 sec 16x25 rest 5 sec	300 2x150 rest 20 sec 4x75 rest 15 sec 6x50 rest 10 sec 12x25
Choice (not Free) <u>Pull</u> <u>Kick</u> <u>Swim</u> no board	300 200 6x25 rest 15 sec	200 200 4x25 rest 15 sec
Swim-down Reverse IM <u>Swim</u>	200	100

Workout II: IM drill, etc + 50s, odds free and even choice		
	3300	2300
Warm-up Free Swim fast turnover with normal distance per stroke	200 200 200 100	200 100 100 100
Mixed Bag Swim Odds Free Evens Choice* Kick Choice Free	16x50 very short rests 300 6x50 on :60	12x50 very short rests 200 6x25 :10 rest
IM Pull any order Drills any order Kick no board Swim usual IM order	400 300 200 100	200 200 200 100
Swim-down Breast Swim exaggerated glide	200	150

* Choice: These are best swum with your worst enemy, who will make the choices for the even numbered 50s.

Workout 12: Straight free + broken choice		
	3400	2400
Warm-up Reverse IM Drill	200	100
Free + Choice Swim		
Free: Count strokes	800	600
Choice (not free, all same)	8x100	6x100
Free: One fewer stroke	400	300
2nd Choice: (not free)	8x50	6x50
Free: Again one fewer stroke	200	100
3rd Choice (nope)	8x25	6x25
Kick Free Choice	100 8x25	100 6x25
Swim-down Choice Drills	100	100

Workout 13: Freestyle + drills, swim & kick Fly, Back, & Breast		
	3000	2000
Warm-up Free Swim First rep at 1000 pace, then each rep 5 sec faster	4x250	4x200
Butterfly Kick no board, front, back, side Drill 1 arm, change each length Swim	200 200 2x100	200 100 2x50
Backstroke Drill Delay pull, kick on side Swim	200 100	100 100
Breaststroke Swim 1 length normal, 1 length dolphin kick	200	100
Freestyle Pull Free, hypoxic: 25 each per 75: 1/3, 1/5, 1/7 Kick	8x75 200	4x75 200
Swim-down Free Drill catch-up	200	100

Workout 14: Freestyle 50s, swim IMs, pull & swim Choice		
	3200	2000
Warm-up Choice Drills	 400	 300
Freestyle Swim Kick	 4x50 on :40 4x50 on :50 4x50 on :60 200 8x25 on :40	 4x50 on :55 4x50 on :65 4x50 on :75 200 4x25 rest 15 sec
IM Swim Fly + Back Fly + Breast Fly + Free IM	 50+150 50+150 50+150 200	 25+75 25+75 25+75 100
Choice Pull least favorite stroke Pull favorite stroke Swim timed	 4x100 4x50 2x100	 4x50 4x25 2x50

Workout 15: Free fartlek; Fly+Free and Back+Breast		
	3000	**2000**
Warm-up Free <u>Swim</u>	500: 1 length easy, 1 hard, 2, 2, 3, 3, 4, 4 500: reverse the above	500: 1 length easy, 1 hard, 2, 2, 3, 3, 4, 4
Fly + Free <u>Swim</u>	100: 25 fl, 75 fr 100: 25 fr, 25 fl, 50 fr 100: 50 fr, 25 fl, 25 fr 100: 75 fr, 25 fl	50: 25 fl, 25 fr 50: fr, fl 50: fl, fr 50: fr, fl
Back + Breast <u>Swim</u> work turns hard	2x150: 100 back, 50 breast 2x150: 50 back, 100 breast	2x100: 75 back, 25 breast 2x100: 25 back, 75 breast
Free <u>Kick</u> <u>Swim</u>	8x50 on :60 8x75+25: moderate 75, 10 sec rest, then hard 25	6x50 on :75 4x75+25: moderate 75, 10 sec rest, then hard 25
Swim-down Free <u>Pull</u>	300	200

Workout 16: Free 50s + Breaststroke		
	3100	2200
Warm-up Choice Swim Kick Pull	 250 250 250	 150 150 150
Freestyle Swim	15x50: 3 each on: :50 :45 :40 :45 :50	10x50: 2 each on: :60 :55 :50 :55 :60
Breaststroke Kick Pull Swim	 150 6x50 150 6x50	 100 4x50 100 4x50
IM Swim	4x125 25 of three, rotating which stroke is 50	4x125 25 of three, rotating which stroke is 50
Swim-down Choice Swim	 200	 150

Workout 17: Long Free warm-up, then IM & Breaststroke		
	3200	**2300**
Warm-up Free Swim	300 3x100 20 sec rest 3x75 15 sec rest 3x50 10 sec rest 3x25 5 sec rest	300 3x100 25 sec rest 3x75 20 sec rest 3x50 15 sec rest 3x25 10 sec rest
IM Swim Fr, Fl, Fr Fr, Ba, Fr Fr, Br, Fr Fl, Ba, Br	 150 150 150 150	 75 75 75 75
Breaststroke Pull Drills Swim	200 200 8x50 on :60	150 150 6x50 on :75
Freestyle Kick Pull count strokes, focus on max DPS*	200, 8x25 200	150 6x25 100
Swim-down Choice Swim	150	100

* DPS: Distance per stroke. Count strokes, focusing on getting maximum distance per stroke.

Workout 18: Free + Butterfly swim, drills, pull, & kick		
	3400	**2100**
Warm-up Choice SKPS	4x150	4x100
Freestyle Swim	8x125 on 1:45	8x75 on 1:45
Butterfly Swim Kick no board; front, back, sides Swim one-arm Kick board; double kick* Swim	4x50 rest time = swim time 100 200 100 8x25 on :45	2x50 rest time = swim time 100 2x100 100 4x25 on :60
IM **Swim**, Kick, Pull, Drill	4x200	4x100
Swim-down Breaststroke Swim count strokes	200	100

* Double kick: Two kicks: First kick begins at chest. The second is smaller, just a hard flip of the ankles. Just as when swimming the whole stroke, get some glide from the kick rather than just kicking frantically.

Workout 19: IM 125s, then Free + broken Choice		
	3100	2500
Warm-up Choice, no rests Swim Kick no board Drills Swim	 200 100 100 100	 200 100 100 100
IM Swim Fl, Fr, Fl Ba, Fr, Ba Br, Fr, Br Fr, Fr, Fr	25 easy, 75 moderate, 25 hard: 125 125 125 125	25 easy, 25 moderate, 25 hard: 75 75 75 75
Free+Choice Swim Free easy Choice hard Free easy Choice harder Free easy Choice hardest Free easy Choice all-out	 400 4x100 300 4x75 200 4x50 100 4x25	 100 4x100 100 4x75 100 4x50 100 4x25
Swim-down Free Swim Catch-up*	 200	 100

* Catch-up: Hand 1 touches Hand 2 stretched out in front before Hand 2 begins to stroke.

Workout 20: Freestyle + IM		
	3200	**2000**
Warm-up		
<u>Swim</u> Free	300	200
<u>Pull</u> IM	200	100
<u>Kick</u> Choice	100	100
Free		
<u>Swim</u> each 5 sec faster	4x250	4x200
<u>Kick</u>	16x25 rest 10 sec	8x25 rest 15 sec
<u>Pull</u> very easy	100	100
IM		
<u>Swim</u> Each 100 is IM, 25 per stroke.	4x125: 1: 100+25 Fly 2: 100+25 Back 3: 100+25 Breast 4: 100+25 Free	4x75: 1: Fl, Ba, Br 2: Ba, Br, Fr 3: Br, Fr, Fl 4: Fr, Fl, Ba
<u>Kick</u> alternate lengths fly & br	200	100
<u>Swim</u> All out	200	100
Swim-Down Choice		
<u>Swim</u>	200	100

Workout 21: Free SKP + IM or Free for triathletes	
3000	
<u>Swim</u> Free	1x200
<u>Swim</u> IM+	2x175: 25 fr, 75 Fl, ba, br, 25 fr
<u>Swim, Kick, Pull</u> Free	3x150
<u>Swim</u> IM+	4x125: 100 IM+25 Stroke (Fl, ba, br, fr)
<u>Pull</u> Free	5x100
<u>Swim</u> IM+	6x75: 3: 1 length each: stroke, free, stroke 3: 1 length each: free, stroke, free
<u>Swim, Kick</u> Free	7x50 SKSKSKS
<u>Swim</u> IM+	8x25 IM on lengths 1, 4, 7; Free on others

Alternately, complete all in freestyle for a workout that's great for triathletes.

Workout 22: 200s and 25s of all strokes		
	3200	2000
Warm-up Choice		
Swim	300	200
Kick	200	100
Pull	100	100
Fly+Free Swim	4x100: Fl, fr, fr, Fl Fl, fr, Fl, fr fr, Fl, fr, Fl fr, Fl, Fl, fr	4x75: Fl, fr, Fl fr, Fl, fr Fl, fr, fr fr, fr, Fl
Kick Fly (no board, prone, sides, supine)	2x100	100
Back Swim	200	200
Kick no board	8x25 rest 10 sec	4x25 rest 15 sec
Swim	8x50 on :60	4x50 on :75
Breaststroke Swim alternate lengths with dolphin & whip kicks	200	100
Swim	8x25 on :40	6x25 on :60
Freestyle Swim	12x50 on :45	8x50 on :70
Swim-down Choice	200	200

	Workout 23: Mostly IMs	
	3000	**2000**
Warm-up Swim + Drills Free + Choice	400: 100 swim 100 catch-up 100 one-arm 100 choice	250 100 swim 75 catch-up 50 one-arm 25 choice
IM Drills Swim IM Free Kick Fl, fr, Bk, fr, Br, fr	200 300 225 ba, br, fr 150 br, fr 75 3x150: 2nd 150 no board	100 4x50 150 ba, br, fr 100 br, fr 50 2x150: 2nd 150 no board
Freestyle Pull easy Swim	200 4x50 on :40 4x50 on :45 4x50 on :50 200	100 4x50 on :40 4x50 on :45 4x50 on :50 100
Swim-down Drill Choice	200	150

Workout 24: Freestyle + IM		
	3400	2300
Warm-up		
Swim Choice	250	150
Drills Free: 1-arm, catch-up, kick (no board), fists, hesitate before recovery	250	150
Freestyle		
Swim	8x125 on 1:30	8x75 on 1:30
Kick	400	200
Pull very easy	100	100
IM 50s are 25 each: Fly, Bk Bk, Br Br, Fr Fr, Fly Swim		
Fly	100	100
IM	4x50	4x50
Back	100	100
IM	4x50	4x50
Breast	100	100
IM	4x50	4x50
Free	100	100
IM	4x50	4x50
Swim-down		
Choice	100	100

Workout 25: Freestyle 250s + IM 25s		
	3200	**2200**
Warm-up Swim Reverse IM Pull Free Swim IM	200 200 100	100 100 100
Freestyle Swim each 5+ sec faster Kick	4x250 250: 10x25 on :30	4x200 150: 6x25 on :45
Choice Pull easy	200	100
IM Swim Fly, Back, Br, Free rest at least 30 sec between groups of 4	8 times 4x25 25's on :30	6 times 4x25 25's on :40
Swim-down Breaststroke Swim minimum number of strokes	200	100

Workout 26: Freestyle 2000 ladder + IM 125s rotating the 50		
	3200	**2400**
Warm-up No rests Swim Free Drills IM Kick IM, no board Swim Choice	 200 100 100 100	 200 100 100 100
Free Swim	4x50 on :45 3x100 on 1:30 2x150 on 2:15 1x200 on 3:00 2x150 on 2:15 3x100 on 1:30 4x50 on :45 2x50 on 1:00	2x50 on :60 2x100 on 2:00 2x150 on 3:00 1x200 2x150 on 3:00 2x100 on 2:00 2x50 on :60
IM Kick Swim	200 4x125 (rotate the 50)	100 4x75: 1: 50 Fly, 25 Bk 2: 50 Bk, 25 Br 3: 50 Br, 25 Fr 4: 50 Fr, 25 Fl
Swim-down Choice Pull	 200	 100

Workout 27: All strokes about equally + Free		
	3000	2100
Warm-up Free Swim first at 800 pace, then each 200 5 sec faster than last	5x200	4x200
Butterfly Kick no board, all sides Drill 1-arm Pull IM 1 length each	200 200 2x100	100 100 2x50
Backstroke Kick & Swim no board, alternate lengths	200	200
Breaststroke Pull Drill: 1 pull, 2 kick, 2 pull, 1 kick, 1 pull, 1 dolphin kick	200 200	100 100
Freestyle Drills: 1-arm, ripple, catch-up, hesitation	200	200
IM Swim	400	200 (rest as needed)
Swim-down Choice	100	100

Workout 28: All strokes about equally		
	3000	2000+
Warm-up Free Swim	500	300
IM + Free Swim	4x50: one of each stroke 3x100: Fl/Bk; Bk/Br, Br/Fr 2x150: Fl, Bk, Br; Bk, Br, Fr 200 IM	4x25: one of each stroke 3x50: Fl/Bk, Bk/Br, Br/Fr 2x75: Fl, Bk, Br; Bk, Br, Fr 100 IM
Kick	300: Free	200: Free
Swim	12x25: 4x Fl, Bk, Br 100: easy IM or Free	12x25: 4 x Fl, Bk, Br 100: easy IM or Free
Choice Pull	4x200 Build-ups*	4x200 Build-ups
Swim-down Breast Drills e.g.,1 pull, 2 kicks; 2 pull,1 kick; 1 pull, 1 fly kick	200	200

* In a buildup, increase the pace steadily throughout the effort. Then for each subsequent effort, you return to the original pace and repeat the increase.

Workout 29: Tons of drills in all strokes		
	3000	**2000**
Warm-up Choice Swim	300	300
Free Swim Time trial Swim: 100s are 5 secs slower than time trial	100 5x100 on 1:30 5x100 on 1:45	100
Butterfly Drills 1 arm, kick with arms behind you, etc. Swim	200 4x25 on :40 4x25 on :45	200 4x25 on :60
Backstroke Drills 1 stroke, kick on side, other arm kick, etc Swim	200 8x25 on :35	200 4x25 on :45
Breaststroke Drills: 1 stroke to 2 kicks; 2 strokes to 1 kick; fly kick Swim	200 8x25 on :40	150 4x25 on :45
Freestyle Drills 1 arm, catch-up, etc Swim	200 8x25 on :30	150 4x25 on :45
Swim-down Cholce Pull	200	100

Workout 30 provides a similar workout without the drills, all swim.

Workout 30: All strokes, no drills	
3000	2500
Freestyle or **Free + IM** Swim: 500	400
4x125 fr or IM & rotate	4x100 free or IM
50	300
400	4x75 (IM without fly)
4x100 free or IM	200
300	4x50 br, fr
4x75 IM without fly	100
200	4x25 fr
4x50 br, fr	
100	
4x25 fr	

Workout 29 provides a similar workout structure with a focus on drills.

Workout 31: Freestyle, IM, Choice		
	3000	**2000**
Warm-up Free <u>Drills</u>: one-arm, ripple, catch-up, choice	400	400
Freestyle + IM <u>Swim</u> Stroke specified, the remainder is Free	200 1st 50 fly 200 2nd 50 back 200 3rd 50 breast 200 IM	100 1st 25 fly 100 2nd 25 back 100 3rd 25 breast 100 IM
Choice (all same) <u>Swim</u>	10x75 Rest 10 sec after first 5	10x50 Rest 15 sec after first 5
Free <u>Pull</u> Alternating 1 length normal breathing, 1 length minimal breathing <u>Swim</u> all-out	500 2x50	400 2x50
Swim-down Free <u>Swim</u> Count strokes	250	200

Workout 32: Lots of Freestyle, a bit of IM, Choice		
	3000	2000
Warm-up Swim Choice Drill Br, one fly kick Swim normal Br Kick IM (no board)	300 150 100 100	200 100 50 100
Freestyle Swim	6x50 on :45 4x100 on 1:30 2x200 on 3:00 4x100 on 1:30 6x50 on : 45	2x50 on :60 2x100 on 2:00 2x150 on 3:00 1x200 on 4:00 2x150 on 3:00 2x100 on 2:00 2x50 on :60
IM Swim	4x125 rotate the 50	4x75: Fly, Bk, Br Bk, Br, Fr Br, Fr, Fly Fr, Fly, Bk
Swim-down Choice Pull	100	100

Workout 33: Freestyle and Backstroke, mostly		
	3000	**2000**
Warm-up Reverse IM Drill or Swim	400	200
Freestyle Swim 5 sec faster per 250	4x250 on 4:00	4x200
Backstroke Drill Swim	150 200 8x25 on :30	100 100 6x25 on :45
Freestyle Kick	300	300
IM Pull Swim Kick no board	300 200 100	2x100 100 100
Swim-down Free Swim	150	150

Workout 34: Freestyle and Breaststroke, mostly		
	3200	**2200**
Warm-up Choice Drill Kick no board Pull	 300 200 100	 200 100 100
Freestyle Swim Time both 200s. Rest 1:00 between 4x50s.	200 timed 4(4x50 on :40) 200 timed	200 2(4x50 on :60) 200
Breaststroke Kick Drill with one dolphin kick Swim with dolphin movement	200 200 8x50 on :50	200 200 6x50 on :70
IM Swim	4x125: 100 IM + 25 stroke	4x100
Swim-down Choice Swim count strokes	100	100

Workout 35: Freestyle Fartlek pyramid + rotating IM 200s		
	3200	**2400**
Warm-up Reverse IM Drills	400	150
Freestyle Swim 1 length easy, 1 hard, 2, 2; 3, 3; 4, 4; 5, 5; 4, 4; 3, 3; 2, 2; 1, 1 Kick Pull relaxed recovery	1250 500 150	1250 300 100
IM Swim Fly, Bk, Br, Free Bk, Br, Free, Fly Br, Free, Fly, Bk Free, Fly, Bk, Br	 200 200 200 200	 100 100 100 100
Swim-down Free Drill	 200	 200

Workout 36: IM + Freestyle		
	3500	**2000**
Warm-up Choice Drills	400	200
IM + Freestyle Swim: 1 slow, 2 moderate, 3 fast	3x300: 100 IM + 200 Fr 3x250: 100 Fl + 150 Fr 3x200: 100 Ba + 100 Fr 3x150: 100 Br + 50 Fr 3x100: All Free	3x200: 100 IM + 100 Fr 3x150: 75 Br + 75 Fr 3x100: 50 Ba + 50 Fr 3x75: 25 Fl + 50 Fr 3x50: All Free
Swim-down Choice Kick no board	200	100

Workout 37: Freestyle 50s, some IM + Worst Stroke 25s		
	3300	**2000**
Warm-up IM Drills	300	200
Freestyle Swim	20x50: 5 on :50 5 on :45 5 on :40 5 on :60	12x50 4 on :60 4 on :55 4 on :70
Choice Kick	500	400
IM Swim mixed order Pull	300 3x100 no rests	200 2x100 no rests
Worst Stroke Swim rest as needed	12x25 attention to technique	8x25 attention to technique
IM Swim	100	100
Swim-down Choice Pull	100	100

Workout 38: Totally IM		
	3000	**2200**
Warm-up IM Kick no board	400	200
Butterfly Swim	4x100 any three lengths fly	4x100 any one length fly
Backstroke Drill Swim	100 4x75	100 4x50
Breaststroke Swim 1 dolphin kick per stroke Normal kick	100 6x50	100 4x50
Freestyle Drill catch-up Swim Kick silent normal	100 12x25 on :20. Rest after 6 200 8x25 :10 rest	100 8x25 on :30. Rest after 4 100 8x25 :15 rest
IM Drill Swim	300 200	200 100
Swim-down Free Swim Count strokes	200	100

Workout 39: Mostly Freestyle, alternating straight and broken		
	3200	**2100**
Warm-up IM Drills	400	300
IM Swim easy Kick no board Swim	300 200 100	100 200 100
Freestyle Swim Alternate easy straight swims with fast broken	400 4x100 on 1:30 300 4x75 on :75 200 4x50 on :50 100 4x25 on :30	300 4x75 on 2:00 200 4x50 on 1:10 100 4x25 on :45
Swim-down Choice Pull	200	200

Workout 40: IM + Stroke		
	3200	**2000**
Warm-up Free Swim	 300	 200
IM Swim easy Kick no board Swim	 300 200 100	 100 200 100
IM + Stroke Swim IM Fly Kick Fly: front, back, sides	 400 4x50 100	 100 4x50 100
Swim IM Back Kick Back: back & sides	300 6x50 on :60 100	100 4x50 on :75 (or one-arm fly) 100
Swim IM Breast Kick Breast: touch heels	200 8x50 on :60 100	100 4x50 on :75 100
Swim IM Free Kick Free: kick silently under water	100 10x50 on :50 100	100 4x50 on :60 100
Swim-down Free Swim Hypoxic 1/5	 200	 200

Workout 41: IM, Breast, & Free		
	3100	**2200**
Warm-up Free <u>Swim</u> normal Fast RPM* Max distance/stroke Fastest style	 100 100 100 100	 100 50 50 100
IM <u>Swim</u>	 4x250 rotate the 100	 4x125 rotate the 50
Breast-stroke <u>Swim</u> single fly kick every other length <u>Swim</u>	 200 8x25 on :35	 100 8x25 on :45
Freestyle <u>Pull</u> <u>Kick</u>	 8x100 15 sec rests 8x25 10 sec rests	 8x100 20 sec rests 8x25 15 sec rests
Choice <u>Swim</u> time trial	 100	 50
Swim-down Choice <u>Drill</u>	 200	 100

* RPM is Revolutions Per Minute. In swimming, this means many strokes rather than the max distance per stroke. Fastest style refers to which of the two (RPM or max distance/stroke) is fastest.

Workout 42: Tons of IM		
	3000	2350
Warm-up <u>Swim</u> nonstop Free Breast Back Fly	200 150 100 50	100 75 50 25
IM <u>Swim</u>	4x250 rotate the 100	4x125 rotate the 50
Stroke + Free <u>Swim</u>	100 Fly + 200 Fr 100 Back + 200 Fr 100 Breast + 200 Fr	50 Fly + 150 Fr 50 Back + 150 Fr 50 Breast + 150 Fr
IM <u>Swim</u> long rests between the sets of 4x25.	4(4x25): rest 5 sec between 25s	4(4x25): rest 10 sec between 25s
Free <u>Kick</u>	200	200
IM <u>Kick</u> rests as above	4(4x25)	4(4x25)
Swim-down <u>Pull</u> hypoxic: 25 each per 75: 1/3, 1/5, 1/7	8x75	4x75

Workout 43: Plenty of freestyle, many drills		
	3400	2500
Warm-up Swim Choice Pull Free Kick Free Swim IM	500 400 300 200	400 300 200 100
Drills Odds: Your choice Evens: My choice*	20x50: rest 10 sec between 50s	20x50 rest 15 sec between 50s
IM Drills Kick Pull Swim	200 200 200 2x100 continuous	100 100 100 100
Swim-Down Free Drills	200	200

* Alternate with a partner, or you can use the below:
Free: kick-head up, return swim head up
Free: underwater recovery
Breast: with free kick
Back: double arm with flutter kick
Free: one-arm, breathe non-stroking side
Fly: kick on each side
Breast: one fly kick, exaggerate motion
Free: one stroke, kick on side, other side
Breast: straight arms
Sit up in water feet first, 'row' with straight arms

Workout 44: Variety		
	3400	**2200**
Warm-up Choice <u>Swim</u>	300	200
IM <u>Swim</u> IM Fly IM Back IM Breast IM Free	250: 100 Fly 8x50: rest 30 sec 250: 100 Back 6x75: rest 25 sec 250 with 100 Breast 4x100: rest 20 sec 250: 100 Free 2x200: rest 15 sec	125: 50 Fly 8x25: rest 30 sec 125: 50 Back 6x50: rest 30 sec 125: 50 Breast 4x75: rest 30 sec 125: 50 Free 2x100: rest 30 sec
Fly <u>Kick</u>	200 8x25 on :30	200 4x25: rest 15 sec
Swim-down Choice <u>Pull</u>	100	100

Workout 45: Tough set of 5 (5x100)		
	3600	**2450**
Warm-up Choice		
Swim	400	100
Kick	300	100
Pull	200	100
Swim	100	50
Free Swim Rest 10 sec between 100s. Rest 1 min between sets.	5(5 x 100): Rest 10 sec between 100s. In each set, swim first 100 comfortably, then each 3 sec faster.	4(5 x 100): Rest 10 sec between 100s. In each set, swim first 100 comfortably, then each 2 sec faster.
Swim-down IM Kick no board	100	100

Workout 46: Relays, for a class or group		
	3000	2000
Warm-up Free Swim Ladder 11 lengths, 10, 9, etc. down to 1	1650 rest 10 sec	1650 rest 20 sec
Kick Choice	350	150
Drills IM	400	200
IM Relays Free	200 200 Another combination	200 200 Another combination
Swim-down Choice Kick no board	200	100

Workout 47: Alternating & rotating stroke IM 100s		
	3300	**2100**
Warm-up Free <u>Swim</u> <u>Kick</u> <u>Pull</u> <u>Swim</u>	 400 300 200 100	 300 200 100 100
IM <u>Swim</u> Fly Fl, Ba; Bk, Br; Br, Fr.	 100 3x100 rest 20 sec	 50 3x50 rest 30 sec
<u>Kick</u> Fly, no board	100	100
<u>Swim</u> Back Ba, Br; Br, Fr; Fr, Fl	100 3x100 rest 20 sec	50 3x50 rest 30 sec
<u>Kick</u> Back, no board	100	100
<u>Swim</u> Breast Br, Fr; Fr, Fl; Fl, Bk	100 3x100 rest 20 sec	50 3x50 rest 30 sec
<u>Kick</u> Breast, no board	100	100
<u>Swim</u> Free Fr, Fly; Fl, Bk; Bk, Br	100 3x100 rest 20 sec	50 3x50 rest 30 sec
<u>Kick</u> Free, no board	100	100
Choice <u>Swim</u> all out, from starting blocks	2x50	2x50
Swim-down Breast <u>Swim</u> long glide	 200	 100

Workout 48: Almost all freestyle; easy pull & hard swim		
	3000	2100
Warm-up Free Swim 5 sec faster per 300	4x300	4x200
Free Pull easy Swim Pull easy Swim Pull easy Swim Pull easy Swim	100 4x25 on :15 100 4x25 on :15 100 4x25 on :15 100 100 all out	100 4x25 on :25 100 4x25 on :30 100 4x25 on :35 100 100 all out
IM Drills Kick Swim	200 200 4x100 no rests	100 100 2x100 no rests
Swim-down Free Drill hesitate before recovery	200	100

Workout 49: Long set of Free 50s + some IM		
	3100	**2400**
Warm-up Choice	400	300
Freestyle Swim	20x50 4 each on: :50 :45 :40 :45 :50	15x50 3 each on: :60 :55 :50 :55 :60
Choice Kick	400	300
IM Swim any order Pull no rests	300 3x100	300 3x100
Worst stroke Swim rest as needed	12x25	10x25
IM Swim hard	200	100
Swim-down Choice Pull	200	100

Workout 50: Freestyle 25s, lots of Backstroke		
	3300	**2200**
Warm-up		
Swim Free	400	300
Drills IM	200	200
Swim Choice	100	100
Freestyle		
Swim	4(6x25 on :20) Rest 40 sec between sets of 6.	4(4x25 on :30) Rest 30 sec between sets of 6.
Backstroke		
Swim	200	100
Kick	200	4x25
Drill	100	100
Swim	8x50 on :60 8x25 on :35	4x50 on :75 4x25 on :45
Pull Easy	100	100
IM		
Kick no back	300	150
Pull	200	100
Swim	100	100
Swim-down Free		
Swim Count strokes	8x25	6x25

Workout 51: Freestyle 50s + IM		
	3300	**2000**
Warm-up Choice Swim & Drills	400	400
Freestyle Swim Kick	15x50: 5 each on :40, :35, :45 300 12x25: 6 each on :25, :35	9x50: 3 each on :55, :50, :60 200 8x25: 4 each on :30, :35
IM Swim: Fl, Bk, Fl Ba, Br, Ba Br, Fr, Br	3x175: 50, 100, 25 3x125: 25, 75, 25 3x75: 25, 25, 25	3x100: 25, 50, 25 3x75: 25, 25, 25 3x25
Swim-down Choice Drills	150	125

Section 5: Triathlon & Ultra-distance

I am proud to say that I'm a drop dead sprinter, preferably butterfly. But I would go to swim meets and sit for 2 hours just to swim for 34 seconds and then sit for 2 hours again. That's no fun! Swimming was what I was good at, but I just wanted to have fun.

You don't sit for 2 hours at the Ironman.

An Ironman is pure fun, it's just a wonderful day. I did 6 Ironmans, so you can imagine I really enjoyed it. It's my favorite length of triathlon.

I got started with triathlon after my husband and I stopped taking long bike trips together. He just didn't want to do them anymore, which I wouldn't argue with. I said to someone, I don't know what to do with myself now, and they said that I could do triathlons. I said, okay!

I had already been swimming, and I built up to do my first triathlon in Baltimore. My second triathlon was the National Championship at Hilton Head. Soon after, I qualified for Ironman, did more national championships, and qualified for World Championship triathlons several times. Triathlons have taken me to places in the world I wouldn't otherwise have gone, like Australia, New Zealand, Switzerland, Cancun, France, and all over the US. At any length of a triathlon, everyone has a weak link and a strong link, which makes for a nice attitude among competitors. We're all friendly with each other, so it is really very pleasant.

Triathlon Basics

Triathlons come in several standard distances, listed in miles below.

	Swim	Bike	Run
Ironman	2.4	112	26.2
Olympic (Standard, World Championship)	0.93	25	6.2
Sprint	0.47	12	3.1
Super-sprint	0.25	6.2	1.6

How long will it take?
Three hours to complete a standard-length triathlon is considered respectable for many triathletes on most terrains. Professionals on a fast course may take under 2 hours to complete a standard triathlon and older racers or a tougher course may take 4 hours.

What do I need?
You only need the essentials: A swimsuit, goggles, the bicycle you already have, an approved helmet, a water bottle, and running shoes. Wondering about socks, shades, shirts, shorts? Many people don't even use them for shorter distances. It could take months to build strength to swim faster, but you can cut your time during the transitions by not towelling off or changing clothes.

Dipping a toe in

Before you enter a triathlon, volunteer as a body-marker for a race near you. Your duty will be over when the athletes are in the water, then you can spend the rest of the time watching how athletes conduct themselves including how they save time during the transitions between events.

Performance

Who needs all those medals, anyway. You don't have to win to enjoy participating, especially your first time. Everyone gets a race number and a teeshirt. Triathlons are some of the most friendly events in the world. It is a party atmosphere, even at the Ironman. Very satisfying. You don't have to devote your whole life to it, and you don't have to dump your family life. Take the family and make a side trip to the zoo. Go with a friend and have a private race within a race.

Minimal Training for Triathlon

So you've decided you'd like to try a triathlon. If you're jumping right up to an Ironman, flip to the next chapter for Ironman training basics and Ironman swim training. If you're doing a standard, sprint, or super-sprint distance, read on.

Overall

The smallest amount of training will consist of 2, preferably 3, sessions per discipline each week. One session of each activity should consist of a straight effort that is longer than the race mileage. For example, if you are training to swim one mile (1500 meters), then swim 2000 meters. Once per week, break that distance into smaller parts and perform it faster than race pace. Once per week, do hills on the bike and run, and concentrate on technique in the swim. Books by Dave Scott and Joe Friel, among others, have extensive advice for all your triathlon training and more advanced triathlon training plans.

Minimum swim training

For most triathletes, the swim is the hard part, and it doesn't have to be. Get in the water for 30 minutes three times per week and change stroke as often as necessary to keep from stopping. Backstroke allows you to breathe as much as you want. Minimize kicking because your quads use a disproportionate amount of oxygen. Every week, reduce the number of laps of strokes other than crawl until you can swim 30 minutes crawl. This will likely take a maximum of 6 weeks.

Rock bottom bike training

One hour twice per week is minimal, but it will do. Vary your speed and learn to spin (pedal quickly) in lower gears. Be sure to include an occasional hill. For longer distance triathlons, aim for 3 rides plus a longer one each week.

Almost no running

Thirty minutes three times per week. Run for 5 or 10 minutes, then walk fast for 15 minutes and run again for the remaining number of minutes. Every week, increase the length of the run, continue to walk some and run the remaining minutes. It should take less than 6 weeks to run a total of 30 minutes.

You may also like a walk-run, in which you pick a ratio of walking to running and gradually increase the length of the runs between walks. For example, you might run 1 minute, walk 4 minutes the first week; run 1:30, walk 3:30 the following week, and so on. You'd complete 6 of these 5-minute segments to equal 30 minutes.

If you're quite new to running, you may like the following: 3 times per week, run a comfortable distance (even if it's a block). Walk back half-way or until you think you can resume running for the rest of the distance. Increase as you are able.

Ironman Basics

I want to finish

Okay. You've got 17 hours for the whole race. 2 hours 20 minutes for the 2.4 mile swim. That leaves you less than 8 hours for the 112 mile bike and another 7 hours to get through the marathon 26.2 run/walk/run/crawl/run.

Everyone says I'm crazy to even think of it

Sure, it's crazy. That's one good reason to do it. And fun. Really fun.

There must be some reason not to do it

Family obligations can be a serious deterrent. It's not good to ignore kids or leave a spouse home alone. Choose races that are near vacation spots and spend extra days there. Get little ones on tricycles or bikes to pedal along beside you when you're running. Go for family swims and bike rides. Tell them what you're doing.

Now tell me why I should do it

It's satisfyingly extreme. The people are supportive. Everyone has a weak link, so you'll be good at something. It does not have the tension of shorter races because the emphasis is on endurance. Go for it!

So how do I even start training?

Take stock of the fitness you already have, and determine what areas you need to build in. See the previous section for info on starting running and biking. The swim is another story. Many triathletes are not spectacular swimmers. Check out the Zero to 700, 1650, and 2.4 plans in this book.

What's the training schedule?
Here's how I did it:
Before breakfast, work, or school for your run, MWFS.
Lunchtime for your swim, MTWRFS.
After work for the bike 4 days, maybe on the same day as the run, or not.

Have fun!

1 to 2.4: Ironman Swim Training

If you can swim one mile, it is easy to increase to 2.4 miles without unusual effort. Begin with a straight swim of 1650 yards or 1500 meters every Monday for a month and add two swim workouts of the same distance per week. If you increase by 500 meters per month, it will take 6 months to reach 2.4 miles. On Fridays, the distance is broken into 10x150, increasing by 50 yards or meters each month so that the final month includes 10x400. This is a long, repetitive set, which is useful in preparing the Ironman swimmer for the mental endurance required. Wednesdays are mentally easier because of their variety and they build strength more efficiently than a distance swim. Wednesday workouts use workout structures described earlier in this book like ladders, pyramids, descending sets, and alternating straight and broken swims. You can find more workouts to include on Wednesdays in the 51 Swim Workouts chapter of this book. If you swim five times per week, then on Tuesdays and Thursdays you can do strokes, drills, running in water, and other generally enjoyable swimming.

Timeline & tapering

The workouts below include instructions for the first month, then separate instructions to extend through months two through six. Plan six months of training before race week. The last week of the final month, swim the 4000 straight on three days. Then, during race week (the Monday, Tuesday, Wednesday leading up to a weekend race), cut back radically to about 1000 yards/meters per day. Two days before the race, do nothing. The day before the race, get in the water long enough to loosen up, not more than 15 minutes, focusing on stretchy movements.

Day	Month 1	Months 2 to 6
Mon	Straight 1500	Increase by 500 each month to 4000
Tue	Various strokes, drills, water run, or no swim	No change in distance
Wed (pick one)	Workout day. Pick one: Ladder 1650 11 lengths, 10, 9, 8, down to 1 (10 sec. rest between) Pyramid 2x50 on :50 (or 5-10 sec rest) 2x100 on 1:45 2x150 on 2:40 2x200 on 3:30 2x150 on 2:40 2x100 on 1:45 2x50 on :50 Descending sets Repeat 5 times: 3x100 For each set of 3, start slowly and go 2 seconds faster each 100. Alternate straight/ broken Repeat 4 times: 150 6x50, 10 sec rest	Workout day. Pick a workout. Increase the total distance by 500 per month, adjusting distances accordingly, for example the below. Pyramid 8x50 6x75 4x100 200 4x100 6x75 8x50 = 2400 200 2x175 3x150 4x125 5x100 6x75 7x50 8x25 =3000
Thur	Same as Tuesday	Remains short and sweet
Fri	10x150	Increase by 50 each month to 10x400

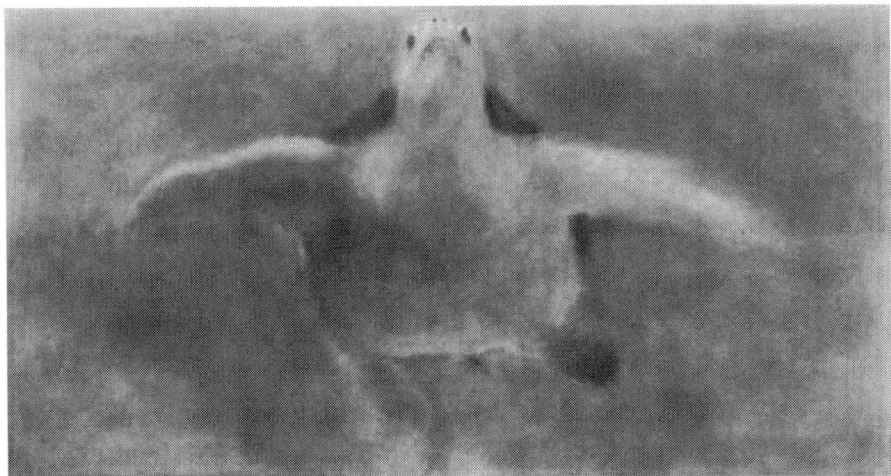

Building to Your First Ultra-distance Swim

Years ago, I helped a few friends prepare for the Great Chesapeake Bay Swim, and a few others joined to train for an ultra-distance for the first time.

Starting out, we were all able to swim a straight mile in around 30 minutes. We decided to swim together once per week, the rest of the week doing our usual workouts of about 2000 yards of mixed strokes.

The general plan was to do a straight swim for time, not distance, once per month, then to do the same approximate length swim, broken into sections, during the other three weeks. We began with one hour, which was about twice our usual distance. All the broken swims included methods like counting strokes, reducing strokes, varying tempo, or technique work, while the straight swims intentionally didn't contain variety to focus on, to train for the sustained mental effort of the actual event. We tapered during the final month while practicing open-water swimming.

While the three who raced were very fast in the pool and in the usual swim of triathlons, this was a whole new game. Between the distance and 50-degree water in June, it was a tough race. When it comes to open water versus the pool, one is all aesthetic, the other is all speed. Outside in open water it's for the aesthetics and that's just great. If you really want to swim fast you have to go into a pool. I like both. I just like water; all of my paintings are full of water.

Using this plan

» SKPDC means swim, kick, pull, drill, choice.

» Distances listed are in meters. Convert as needed.

Mo	Wk	Weekly shared workout (meters)
1	1	3000 meters, Slow, straight, any stroke
	2	1500 + 10x150 SKPDC
	3	1500 + 100, 200, 300, 400, 300, 200, 100
	4	1500 + 4x200, 4x100, 4x75, 4x25
2	1	4000
	2	2000 + 10x200 SKPDC
	3	2000 + 400, 4x100, 300, 4x75, 200, 4x50, 100, 4x25
	4	2000 + 8x50, 4x100, 400, 4x100, 8x50
3	1	5000
	2	2500 + 10x250 SKPDC
	3	2500 + 500, 2x250, 4x125, 5x100, 10x50
	4	2500 + 10x50, 5x100, 500, 5x100, 10x50
4	1	6000
	2	3000 + 10x300 SKPDC
	3	3000 + 200, 2x175, 3x150, 4x125, 5x100, 6x75, 7x50, 8.25
	4	3000 +500, 10x100, 10x75, 10x50, 10x25,
5	1	7000
	2	3500 + 10x350 SKPDC
	3	3500 +600, 12x50, 500, 10x50, 400, 8x50, 300, 4x50
	4	3500 + 1x350, 2x300, 3x250, 4x200, 5x150, 6x100, 7x50
6	1	2 hours open water, local lakes
	2	1 hour thirty minutes, open water, local lakes
	3	1 hour, open water, local lakes
	4	Race day: 7500 meters / 4.4 miles

Section 6: Etcetera

Just a little more. In this section, you'll find some brief answers to some common questions and my record of the races I've competed in over the years.

Quick Questions

Walk me through what will happen the first time I go to the pool.
Friends are made.

Is the pool different at different times of day?
No. Check the schedule to see when you're allowed to swim. Ask pool staff for help if you'd like.

Sharing lanes
Up one side, back the other. Usually on the left (clockwise).

Where do I put my stuff?
Locker.

Do you find it a hassle to go to the pool, change, shower, etc? How do you deal with that?
No.

Glasses, contacts, medical devices.
Pacemaker under skin should be no problem. Insulin pumps can be temporarily taken off. But ask your doctor about how to swim with your medical device. Put your glasses in your locker or take to the end of your lane in a case. Contacts under goggles are likely ok, but ask your doctor.

Goggles
Yes.

Will I get sucked into the drain?
Of course. All skinnies disappear. Ha.

Will I get an infection in a pool?
Nah.

When not to swim
Don't swim with illness, injury, cuts, etc.

Showering before swimming in a pool
Rinse off icky sweat.

Swim cap
Yes, use a swim cap, especially if hair is long.

Tips for getting water in your mouth and handling waves
Don't swallow.

Goggles under cap or over
Goggles over cap.

Wearing a watch while swimming
I don't.

Gauging direction and location in open-water swimming
Open eyes, often.

On being an athlete who is older and a woman
Focusing on my age and gender is not needed.

Nose clip
Never, I exhale through my nose.

Earplugs
I don't think I would like that.

Wetsuits
You wear a wetsuit if it's allowed. The race has a temperature cutoff. I'm very weak about cold, I have a problem with cold water, my skin will turn red. In New Zealand, it was 57 degrees and I had to stay on my back a lot because it was unbreathable.

A wetsuit is actually a flotation device, so it speeds up the swimming for everyone. Because of that, I would always prefer that the race would be without wetsuits. I wanted it more than anyone else, but everyone else benefited from it more than I did.

Prepping for a race

I'd do some slow, easy, stretchy stuff the day before the race. That was my general rule. Two days before a race I don't do anything and there's a reason for that. If you have a hard workout or race, notice how you feel fine the next day and exhausted the second day. I took that wisdom and made sure that two days before the race I did nothing and it worked.

Do you get nervous or have trouble sleeping from excitement the night before a race?

No.

Setting goals

Sure. Ironman was a goal. You have to have that as a goal in order to do it.

Sleep

I just get the usual 7 or 8 hours and I'm not usually tired.

Food and body shape

Food has never been a technical thing for me. I like to eat, and I eat whatever I like, just nothing in great quantities. If something is supposed to be not good for you I not only eat it anyway but I generally find out eventually that they changed their minds and it really is good for you.

I was born a little bit skinny and my mother tried very hard to plump me up but it never worked. She was right. If you get sick, you could lose weight, so it's good to have a little extra weight on you. I had a scale, but the battery wore out and I never replaced it. I never focused on my body shape. I never had to and I still don't. I don't think that would be a fun thought.

Would you have done anything differently in your life?

If there was something I could have done differently, I did it. I've made big changes without hesitation.

Did you have role models?

No.

Building confidence

I've always been confident. It came naturally.

Appendix: Races and Times

Photo of Ruth (author) in the ITU Triathlon World
Championships in Lausanne, 1998
Image courtesy of the author

Swimming Competitions

Date	Place	FR50	FR100	FR200	FR500	FLY50
79 - 10/27 (Age 49)	York Pa	36:62 2nd			8:30 1st	40:59 2nd
79 - 11/18	Newark De	35:44 2nd		3:03:54 2nd	8:14:75 1st	39:59 2nd
80 - 1/27	Wash: DC	34:60 1st		3:05 1st		38:80 1st
80 - 2/16-17	Balt Md	34:26 1st		3:01:20 1st	8:11:27 1st	37:20 1st
80 - 3/19	Berwyn Pa	34:81 1st	1:20:82 1st			39:06 1st
80 - 4/19-20	York Pa	33:64 1st		2:59:68 1st	8:00:50	37:03 1st
80 - 5/23-25	Y Nat: York Pa	33:95 1st	1:17:09 1st	2:56:90 1st	7:57:91 1st	38:05 2nd
80 - 10/18	York Pa	34:63 1st	1:18:62 1st			37:16 1st
80 - 11/16	Cornell, Ithaca NY	34:12 1st		2:58:08 1st		37:31 1st
80 - 11/23	Newark De	33:74 1st			7:57:31 1st	36:78 1st
81 - 1/24	Wash DC	32:90 1st	1:16:70 1st			36:04 1st
81 - 3/22	Berwyn Pa	33:40 1st	1:15:80 1st			35:74 1st
81 - 4/4	Catons Md					
81 - 4/12	Cornell, Ithaca NY	32:97 1st			7:43:97 1st	35:49 1st
81 - 4/25	York Pa	32:59 1st			7:32:35 1st	35:07 1st
81 - 5/16-17	Y Nats Westport	32:95 meet R	1:13:95 meet R	2:48:53 meet R	7:41:12 meet R	35:34 meet R
81 - 8/13-16	L:C: Nats Canton	37:08 1st	1:23:32 1st	3:10:09 1st	6:47:20 2nd	41:04 1st
81 - 9/20	Cornell, Ithaca NY	33:65 1st				35:47 1st
81 - 10/24-25	York Pa	31:70 1st		2:46:29 1st	7:28:73 1st	34:38 1st
81 - 11/22	Newark De	32:74 1st				36:25 1st
82 - 2/27	Balt Md	1:13:50 1st			7:31:90 1st	36:67 1st
82 - 3/27	Balt Md					
82 - 4/4	Newark De	32:71 1st	1:14:73 1st			36:36 1st

Swimming Competitions (contd.)

Date	Place	FR50	FR100	FR200	FR500	FLY50
82 - 5/8-9	Y Nats WV	31:68 meet R	1:13:58 meet R	2:54:14 1st	7:44:00 1st	35:77 1st
82 - 8/7-8	Naval A: LC	37:03 1st		1:25:29 1st		
82 - 8/14-15	Nat: Sp: Phila Pa	32:46 1st		1:13:85 1st		36:32:00
82 - 10/30	York Pa	32:84 1st	1:14:76 1st		7:39:23 1st	35:93 1st
82 - 11/21	Newark De	32:74 1st				36:73 1st
83 - 1/9	Easton Pa	32:03 1st				36:76 1st
83 - 2/26	Balt Md	32:64 1st		2:49:78 1st	7:44:15 1st	36:12 1st
83 - 3/20	Berwyn Pa	33:63 1st	1:14:50 1st			37:73 1st
83 - 3/27	Newark De		1:13:62 1st			36:78 1st
83 - 4/23	York Pa	32:79 1st			7:35:10 1st	36:18 1st
83 - 5/13	Y Nats Chicago	32:61 1st	1:13:46 new R	2:55:80 1 new R	7:38:10 new R	36:45 1st
83 - 8/6-7	Balt Md LC	37:32 1st	1:25:47 1st	3:14:00 1st	6:50:36 1st	41:80 1st
83 - 9/25	Carlisle Pa	32:90 1st			7:36:79 1st	38:19 1st
83 - 10/22	York Pa	33:16 1st			7:32:79 1st	37:96 1st
83 - 11/20	Newark De	32:20 1st				37:30 1st
83 - 1/24	Berwyn Pa	32:97 1st	1:14:62 1st		7:37:15	37:56 1st
84 - 1/29	Easton Pa	32:14 1st	1:15:98 1st	2:49:10 1st		38:45 1st
84 - 2/25	Balt Md		1:14:00 2nd			41:15 2nd
84 - 3/18	Berwyn Pa	33:14 1st				36:92 1st
84 -3/31	Towson Md					
84 - 4/28	York Pa	33:55 1st	1:17:00 1st		7:40:12 1st	38:89 1st
84 - 9/23	Carlisle Pa	32:87 1st				37:46 1st
84 - 10/20	York Pa	33:66 1st			7:36:00 1st	36:90 1st
84 - 11/18	Newark De	33:63 1st				36:70 1st

Swimming Competitions (contd.)

Date	Place	FR50	FR100	FR200	FR500	FLY50
85 - 1/27	Easton Pa	33:46 1st		2:55:95 1st		39:00 1st
85 - 3/10	Balt Md					
85 - 4/27	York Pa	32:90 1st	1:14:09 1st			36:60 1st
85 - 9/8	Toronto LC	36:99 2nd	1:23:88 3rd	3:15:10 5th		48:77 5th
85 - 9/22	Dicken-son Pa	33:78 1st				38:15 1st
85 - 10/26	York Pa	33:56 1st				38:15 1st
85 - 11/24	Newark Pa	33:09 1st				37:31 1st
86 -3/16	Balt Md					
86 - 4/13	York Pa	33:64 1st		2:53:00 1st		38:01 1st
86 - 4/26	Indiana-polis Pa	33 1st	1:18 1st			43:27 2nd
87 - 3/26	Newark De					
87 - 10/24	York Pa	35:69 1st			7:58 1st	37:94 1st
87 - 11/22	Newark	36				39

Running Races

Date	Location	Distance	Time	Place
83 - May 30 (Age 52)	Boalsburg Memorial Day Race	4mi	32:48	1st over 50
84 - July 15	Arts Festival	10mi	87:30	1st over 50
85 - May 27	Boalsburg Memorial Day	4mi	32:22	1st over 50
85 - July 14	Arts Festival	10mi	86:16	1st over 50
86 - July 13	Arts Festival	10k	53:34	1st over 50
87 - Sept 6	Labor Day	5k	23:55	1st over 40
88 - May 30	Boalsburg	4mi	29:33	1st over 50
88 - July 10	Arts Festival	10k	50:28	1st over 45
88 - Sept 5	Labor Day Race	5k	23:55	1st over 50
89 - March 12	Campus Run-around	5k	24:07	1st over 50
89 - July 16	Arts Festival	10k	49:46	1st over 50
89 - Sept 4	Labor Day	5k	24:20	1st over 50
90 - March 11	Campus Run-around	5k	24:07	1st over 50
90 - May 30	Boalsburg	4mi	30:46	1st over 50
90 - July 15	Arts Festival	10k	50:16	1st over 50
90 - Sept 3	Labor Day	5k	24:56	1st over 40
91 - March 17	Campus Run-around	5k	25:07	1st over 50
91 - April 6	CC Hosp (superhills)	5k	25:35	1st over 50
91 - May 12	Nike Mother's Day Wash DC	8k	39:15	2nd 60+
91 - May 27	Boalsburg	4mi	31:09	1st over 50
91 - July 4	Peachtree Classic, Atlanta	10k		
91 - July 14	Arts Festival	10k	53:54	1st over 50
91 - Sept 2	Labor Day	5k	24:42	1st over 50
91 - Sept 14	Corporate (Supelco)	5k	25:07	1st over 40
92 - March 29	Avia Ladies Baltimore	10k	51:27	1st over 60
92 - April 4	CC Hosp (superhills)	5k	25:14	1st over 50
92 - May 11	Nike Mother's Day Wash DC	8k	39:51	1st over 50
92 - May 23	Moshannon Y (mountain)	10k	55:54	1st over 50
92 - July 12	Arts Festival	10k	53	1st over 60

Triathlons

Date	Location/ event	Swim	Bike	Run	Total
1987					
June 28 (Age 56)	Baltimore, USTS	1.5k	40k	10k	3.02:38 AG2
		31:31 (3:15)	1.33 (2:13)	52.34	
Sept 20	Hilton Head (Nat'ls)	1.5k	40k	10k	2:46:11 AG4
		23:01 (2:33)	1:25:45 (2:03)	52:49:00	
1988					
May 1	Miami, USTS	1.5k	40k	10k	2:57:54 AG1
		31:43 (3:04)	1:29:53 (2:16)	50:58:00	
June 25	Baltimore, USTS	1.5k	40k	10k	3:04:21 AG2
		33.31 (2:54)	1:30:57 (3:02)	53:57:00	
July 16	Tupper Lake, Tinman	2000m	56mi	13.1mi	6:41:18 AG1
		45.1	3:46	2:10:08	
Sept 4	Wilkes Barre (Nat'ls)	1500m	40k	10k	3:17:47 AG3
		33:08 (2:18)	1:43:06 (4:00)	54:41:00	
Oct 22	Hawaii, Ironman	2.4mi	112mi	26.3mi	15:26:07 AG3
		1:31	8:00	6:00	
1989					
June 25	Columbus	1.5k	40k	10k	2:55 AG1
Aug 11	Avignon (Worlds)	2000m	40k	10k	
					3:10:37 AG3
Aug 18	Winchester	.5mi	17mi	5mi	2:04:55 AG1
		16:29 (3:00)	1:00:38 (1:46)	43:02:00	
Nov	Florida, (Nat'ls)	.5mi	13mi	3.1mi	1:21:13 AG1
		16:00 (2:27)	1:38:08	24:37:00	
1990					
June 24	Baltimore, USTS	1.5k	40k	10k	3:08:03 AG2
		29:22 (4:37)	1:35:09 (2:41)	56:14:00	
July 28	Akron, Bally's Scand. Spa	1k	40k	10k	2:45 AG1

Triathlons (contd.)					
Date	Location/ event	Swim	Bike	Run	Total
Aug 12	Leon's (Nat'ls)	1.5k	40k	10k	2:45 AG3
Aug 19	Winchester	.5mi	17mi	5mi	2:02 AG1
		16:09 (1:38)	58:19 (1:19)	45:16	
Sept 15	Disneyland (Worlds)	1mi	25mi	6.2mi	2:56:15 AG2
		31:49 (2:49)	1:22:47 (1:59)	56:51	
1991					
June 23	Baltimore, Budlight	1mi	25mi	6.2mi	3:04:28 AG2
		34:51 (3:12)	1:26:46 (3:53)	55:46:00	
June 30	Columbus, Budlight	1mi	25mi	6.2mi	2:40:34 1st over 50
		30:34 (2:34)	1:12:12 (1:49)	53:25:00	
July 28	Leon's (Nat'ls)	1mi	25mi	6.2mi	3:12 AG3
Aug 25	Chicago Sun Times (triathlon PR)	1mi	22mi	6.2mi	2:36:44 1st over 50
		29:58 (4:49)	1:06 (2:02)	53:44:00	
Sept 8	Lancaster, YMCA	.5mi	15mi	5mi	2:00:42 1st over 50
		17:52	56:04	46:42	
Oct 13	Australia (Worlds)	1.5k	40k	10k	2:56:37 AG3
		35:35	1:24:26	56:34	
1992					
June 14	Wilmington	1.5k	40k	10k	2:49:45 AG1
		29:39 (2:53)	1:15:47 (1:32)	59:54	
June 28	Columbus	1.5k	40k	10k	2:52:54 377/600+
		30:08 (4:10)	1:22	55	
July 18	Tupper Lake	1.2mi (63 deg)	56mi	13.1mi	6:51 AG1
		41	3:39	2:23	
Aug 2	Cleveland	1.5k	40k	10k	2:55:12 AG2 760/798
		33:22 (1:23)	1:25:21 (1:21)	53:44:00	

Triathlons (contd.)

Date	Location/ event	Swim	Bike	Run	Total
Aug 16	Wilkes Barre	1.5k	40k	10k	3:16:40 AG1
		33 (3:24)	1:30 (1:39)	1:09:01	
Sept 12	Muskoga (Worlds)	1.5k (62 deg)	40k	6.2mi	3:20:58 AG2
		34	1:40	57	
Oct 10	Hawaii, Ironman	2.4mi	112mi	26.2mi	16:21:29 AG2
		1:21:23	7:56:23	7:03:43	
1993					
June 4	Edinburgh	.6mi	23mi	6.2mi	2:51:06 32/40 AG1
		20.02 (2:24)	1:20:30 (18.5)	1:56	
Jul 17	Columbus	1500 meters	22mi	6.2mi	2:58 AG1/2
		33	1:21	1:09	
Aug 14	Columbia (Nat'ls)	1.5k	41k	10k	3:22:29 AG 3/8
		32:59:00	1:32:53	1:42	
1995					
May 21	Memphis in May	1.5k	25k	6.2mi	2:55:02 AB 1/2
		27:19 (2:11)	1:18:27 (18:7)	1:05:02	
June 25	Columbus	.5k	18.5k	4k	1:57:10 AG 1/2
		17:18 (2:17)	55:09 (1:46)	40:40:00	
July 16	Akron	0.5k	17k	4k	1:52:30 AG 1/1
		13:50 (2:12)	55:12:00 (1:55)	39:11 (9:48)	
Aug 27	Chicago (Nat'ls)	1.5k	25k	6.2mi	3:07:13 AG 2/6
		33:29 (2:31)	1:21:50 (2:28)	1:06:45	
Oct 7	Hawaii, Ironman	2.4mi	112mi	26.2mi	
		1:25	9		
Nov 11	Cancun	1950m	25mi	6.2mi	4:13 AG 3/6
		39 (3:32)	1:18:06 (e:42)	1:08:43	
1996					
May 19	MeMphis in May	1.5k	25k	6.2mi	3:07:23 AG 1/1
		29:40 (1:19)	1:21:30 (2:21)	1:12:35	

Triathlons (contd.)					
Date	Location/ event	Swim	Bike	Run	Total
June 16	Springfield, Ironhorse	1.5mi / 52:05:00	45mi / 2:40:10	10mi / 2:23:06	5:55:38 AG 1/1
June 23	Orange County (Nat'ls)	1.5k / 28:07 (1:39)	26k / 1:33:55 (1:58)	6.2mi / 1:11:25	3:17 AG 2/6
July 21	Baltimore, Danskin	.5mi / 16:48 (2:01)	11mi / 36:04 (1:49)	3.1mi / 31:49:00	1:28:31 AG 1/2
Aug 25	Cleveland (Worlds)	1.5k / 35:48 (2:45)	25k / 1:19:15 (3:02)	6.2mi / 1:07:47	3:08:31 AG 2/6
Oct 26	Hawaii, Ironman	2.4mi	112mi	26.2mi	
Nov 27	Wellington (Worlds)	1500 m / 35:01:00	25mi / 1:50:11	6.2mi / 1:07:39	3:32:05 AG3/7
1997					
May 18	Memphis in May	1.5k / 28:18 (2:02)	25k / 1:35:58 (2:39)	6.2mi / 1:19:52	3:28
June 15	Springfield, Ironhorse	1.5mi / 53:31:00	45mi / 2:50:53	10mi / 2:23:12	6:07:35
June 29	Columbus, Wendy's	.5mi / 20:32	19.5mi / 57:09	4mi / 41:40	2:00:23 AG 1/1
July 20	Baltimore, Danskin	.5mi / 17:12	11mi / 2:27:35	3.1mi / 30:20	1:27:29 AG 1/3
Aug 17	Columbia (Nat'ls)	1mi / 31:39:00	25mi / 1:28	6.2mi / 1:09	3:14:29 AG 1/3
Sept 7	Reston, VA	1mi / 33:33 (2:41)	23mi / 1:13:14 (1:34)	6.2mi / 1:06:48	2:57:48 1st over 50
Oct 19	Hawaii, Ironman	2.4mi / 1:25:50	112mi / 8:41:29	26mi / 6:31:40	16:38:59 2nd over 65
1998					
May 17	Memphis in May	1.5k / 29:54:00	25k / 1:29:04	6.2mi / 39:39:00	3:19 2nd over 65
June 21	Florida (Nat'ls)	1.5k / 32:28:00	25k / 1:40:11	6.2mi / 1:11:45	3:29 AG 2/5

Triathlons (contd.)

Date	Location/event	Swim	Bike	Run	Total
July 12	Akron, Ohio	.5mi	17k	4k	1:57:34 AG 1/1
		14:41 (2:02)	55:53 (1:41)	43:07:00	
Aug 30	Lausanne (Worlds)	1.5k	25k	6.2mi	2:29:15 1/4 w
		33:27 (3:56)	1:49:04 (2:37)	1:10:08	
Sept 13	Reston, VA	1.5k	25k	6.2mi	3:08 1/2
		35:23 (1:26)	1:14:54 (1:32)	1:14:47	
1999					
May 23	Memphis in May	1.5k	25k	6.2mi	3:13:39 2nd over 65
		30:32 (1:47)	1:22:55 (2:26)	1:17:01	
June 6	Blackwater Eagleman	2k	56k	13.2mi	7:45 1/2
		51:17 (3:09)	3:19 (2:34)	3:28	
July 18	Atlanta, USTS	1.5k	25k	6.2mi	3:07:47 1/1
		33:42 (1:30)	1:20:22 (1:47)	70:27:00	
July 25	Bridgeton (Sprints Nat'ls)	.5mi	16k	3.1k	1:51:44 1/1
		17:48	1:00:12	33:46:00	
Sept 12	Reston, VA	1.5k	25k	6.2mi	3:07:53 2/3
		35:44 (1:32)	1:16:41 (2:12)	1:11:44	
Oct 23	Hawaii, Ironman	2.4mi	112mi	26.2mi	16:47:15 2/4
		1:28	8:21	6:49	
2000					
May 21	Memphis in May	1.5k	25k	6.2mi	3:21:26 1/2
		32:32 (2:01)	1:24:52 (2:48)	1:19:14	
July 15	Muncie, IN	2k	56k	13.2k	8:00:45 1/1
		50:33 (3:25)	3:43	3:20	
Sep 9	St.Joe's (Nat'ls)	1.5k	25k	6.2mi	3:40:13 3/4
		31:28 (2:40)	1:47:57	1:16:19	
2001					
May 20	Memphis in May	1.5k	25k	6.2mi	3:13:41
		30:32	1:21:55	1:17:01	

Triathlons (contd.)					
Date	**Location/ event**	**Swim**	**Bike**	**Run**	**Total**
2002					
June 9	Austin, Danskin	.25k 16:08	11k 48:24	2k 35:25	1:43:47 1/2
2003					
May 18	Orlando, Danskin	.25k 9:01	11k 37:26	2k 23:17	1:13:03 1/1
June 29	Columbus	.5k 17:12 (2:17)	18.5k 1:10:10 (2:43)	3.1k 38:53	2:11:15 1/1
2004					
June 27	Columbus	.5k 15:43 (2:31)	18.5k 1:13:11 (2:40)	3.1k 41:29	2:15:00 1/1
2005					
August 6	Canoe Creek	.5k 17:16 (2:45)	12.67k 51:48 (1:28)	3.2k 40:00	1:54:00 1/1
Sept	New York, Danskin	.25k 18:21 (3:15)	11k 39:10 (1:40)	2k 40:01	1:41:29 1/1
2006					
July 9	Philly, Women's	.5mi 13:19 (1:06)	16k 1:03:15 (1:43)	2k 41:39	2:01:01 1/1
Aug 5	Canoe Creek	.5k 18:12 (2:19)	13k 56:58 (1:26)	3.2k 41:52	2:00:47 1/1
Aug 27	Columbia, Irongirl	1k 22:22 (2:15)	30k 1:17:17 (1:56)	3k 46:19	2:30:07 1/1
2007					
June	Pittsburgh	1k 36:40 (1:38)	16k 1:59:19 (1:32)	6.2mi 1:24:55	4:04:00
August	Canoe Creek	.5k 18:03 (2:45)	13k 53:47 (2:32)	3.2k 40:39	1:57:46
August	IronGirl	1k 24:58 (2:35)	30k 1:19:24 (1:07)	3k 29:29	2:33:46

Triathlons (contd.)					
Date	Location/ event	Swim	Bike	Run	Total
2008					
July 6	State College	.5k	13k	3.2k	1:52:07
		13.34	53:01	41:40	
Aug 2	Canoe Creek	.5k	13k	3.2k	2:04:00
		17:58 (2:44)	59:17 (1:40)	42:46	
2009					
July 5	State College	.5k	13k	3.2k	1:58:15
		18:10 (1:21)	53:51 (2:14)	40:40	
July 22	IronGirl Columbia	1k	30k	3k	2:38:12 1/1
		25:05 (2:57)	1:20:28 (2:31)	47:13	
Sep	Washington DC	1k	30k	3k	3:52:19
		37:08 (3:30)	1:40:12 (3:03)	1:28:29	
2010					
July 3	State College	.5k	13k	3.2k	1:49:33
		18:50	48:43	38:34	

Rachel (editor) and Ruth (author) in State College, July 2021
Image courtesy of Sybilla Beckmann Kazez (daughter-in-law)

Photo of Ruth (author) by Marc Freeman (date unknown)
Image courtesy of the author

About This Book

Thank you for reading! We are delighted to bring this book into the world and hope you have found it useful.

The core information and workouts in this book are material from www.ruthkazez.com from 2000-2020, edited by Rachel Kazez (granddaughter) in Fall 2021. Memoir sections, introductions, and instructions for using the workouts and book were created by Rachel from an interview on Zoom between Rachel and Ruth on October 12, 2021 and from ongoing conversation via email and family Zoom calls. Paintings and drawings were created by Ruth. Photos are as listed. Becky Groves (granddaughter) laid out the art and prepared the document for publishing in Fall 2021. Jean Kazez (daughter) provided a read-through, coordinated throughout the process, and typed the race times appendix from records Ruth kept and posted on her website. Correspondence about this book can be directed to Rachel Kazez.

Ruth Kazez (author & artist) is an artist and athlete living in State College, Pennsylvania. Her art has been exhibited across the country. Her swimming, biking, and running have taken her across the world in competitions, and her popular swim workout website www.ruthkazez.com has attracted over 12 million hits. This is her first book. Find her at www.ruthkazez.com.

Rachel Kazez (editor), Ruth's granddaughter, is an endurance sports enthusiast who lives in Chicago and works in clinical social work. Rachel shares Ruth's love of athletics, being outdoors, and making art. This is her first published book. Find her at www.rachelkazez.com.

Becky Groves is Jean's daughter and works as a software engineer in Pittsburgh.

Jean Kazez is Ruth's daughter and teaches philosophy in Dallas.

Printed in Great Britain
by Amazon